Charles Wesley Leffingwell

Lyrics of the Living Church

Charles Wesley Leffingwell

Lyrics of the Living Church

ISBN/EAN: 9783744783354

Printed in Europe, USA, Canada, Australia, Japan

Cover: Foto ©Thomas Meinert / pixelio.de

More available books at **www.hansebooks.com**

LYRICS

OF

THE LIVING CHURCH

♦riginal ♯oems

COMPILED FROM "THE LIVING CHURCH"

/EDITED BY

C. W. LEFFINGWELL

CHICAGO

A. C. McCLURG AND COMPANY

1891

Preface.

THE editor of "THE LIVING CHURCH," during the first decade of its publication, was several times requested to preserve in book form the best of the verses which had appeared in its columns; and a literary friend in New York having submitted for consideration a number of selections, properly classified, the enterprise was decided upon.

In so large a field to glean from, it is more than probable that some grain has been overlooked. There may have been errors of judgment in making the selections, even though the editor has tried to please a great variety of readers rather than in all respects to please himself. If there are any verses which seem to some unworthy of a place, perhaps to others these verses will be prized as the best in the book. It is hoped that all will here find something to edify and nothing to offend.

To the handsome setting which the publishers propose to give THE LYRICS, the illustrations will add a charm. A few of them will be recognized as drawings from the old masters; the greater part are original designs.

The number of writers being so large, and the addresses of many being unknown, it has not been practicable to send proof for correction. Any errors to which the editor's attention is called will be corrected in future editions, if such editions shall be demanded, and names of writers not here given will be added, if desired.

THE EDITOR.

CHICAGO, A.D. 1891.

Contents.

LIST of Illustrations

DRAWN BY

J. H. GRATACAP.

Headpieces.

List of Authors.

2

The Christian Year.

TO MY CALENDAR.

By Margaret A. Mylrea.

THE calendar hangs in my quiet room,
　　'Neath the picture on the wall,
Where the morn's pale light, and the evening gloom,
　　In softened shadows fall.

It tells the days of the Christian life, —
　　Events, as they come and go :
The hero's birth, and the martyr's strife,
　　The seasons as they flow.

It speaks in a monotone to me,
　　Of the fleeting, fading hours;
How time's dark wheel turns ceaselessly,
　　Amid life's brightest flowers.

I turn the page as the morning song
　　Floats over the eastern sea ;
I join in the glad earth's chanting throng —
　　" Most Holy ! One in Three ! "

And when the day is worn and spent —
When midnight musings come,
I close the leaf; I have pitched my tent
One day's march nearer home.

Old friend! thou wilt hang on my silent wall,
Thy earthly records keep,
While morning and evening shadows fall
Upon my dreamless sleep.

May I, when loosed is the silver cord,
Without one single plea
But Thy shed Blood, say, " Here, O Lord,
And those Thou gavest me !"

THE CIRCLE OF THE SANCTUARY.

By W. B. Chisholm.

ALL times are thine, Church of the Living God,
And Pillar of the Truth!
Be these thy sacred vestibules still trod,
While yet in ruddy youth
The new year rings with its dead fellow's dirge,
E'en to its own last verge,
The stars and wreaths of Christmas, and the rose
That 'gainst the sunburst of His Rising glows;
For every feast, for every fast, its niche
In pious hearts, and thus she doth beseech
Of those yet leal unto her holy bond
That they in spirit and in form respond
E'en to the days of her sepulchred saints;
These with their holy plaints
And grateful pæans followed her bright way:
Be we as true in this her brighter day!

THE LORD'S DAY.

By Marah.

A PEACEFUL stillness broods o'er all the scene,
  A holy quietness that speaks of rest ;
The air is fresh, the heavens look down serene,
  The sun moves slowly onward toward the west.

The harvest fields of gently waving grain,
  The ripening fruits that glisten in the sun,
Remind us of the merry reapers' strain,
  And speak of labor that has wrought and won.

But on this quiet Sunday afternoon,
  This day to us most blest of all the seven,
We banish cares that will return full soon,
  And raise our hearts and turn our thoughts to Heaven.

It is a season for reflective thought,
  For meditation free and unconfined ;
The very air with peacefulness seems fraught,
  That stills the nerves and soothes the troubled mind.

Now stealing o'er us comes a holy calm ;
  Our burdens and our cares are lost in love ;
And from our lightened hearts we raise a psalm
  Of praise and gratitude to God above.

And, musing thus, we wonder more and more
  Our Father's love can bear with us so long ;
That He who all our sins and sorrows bore
  Should at our hands receive such cruel wrong.

We know He orders all things for our good ;
  And yet, how oft we murmur at His will,
And in a thankless and complaining mood
  Receive the blessings which our being fill !

But see! The shadows lengthen. daylight fades:
In thoughts like these, the day has passed away.
But, as we watch the twilight's deepening shades,
We thank " Our Father " for this blessed day.

And from our hearts a fervent prayer ascends
That, in the coming days and months and years,
We may to Him whose wisdom shapes our ends
Give love and gratitude, not doubts and fears.

IN CHURCH TIME.

BY THE REV. R. W. LOWRIE, D.D.

[Imitation of Herbert.]

WHEN rings the church bell, then, be on thy way,
    Not at thy glass,
        As many are, alas !
    It were, indeed, a sin
    To lose Confession for a final pin !
Decently dressed — not gaudily, I pray :
    Go not in state,
        Nor linger at the gate :
But, eager for the blessings kept in store,
Pass porchway through, and seek the church's door ;
    And when thereat,
        Lift heart as well as hat ;
And, kneeling, do thou kneel and use each knee,
On stool or floor, in all humility.

Be mindful. ever, 't is the house of prayer,
    And, prayer, a key, —
        Though passing strange it be, —
    That turned in ward aright,
        Discovers wealth. exceeding India's quite ;
Not two or three resort but God is there ;

Then mindful be
Of His Divinity,
And, in such presence, of thyself be ware,
And have all reverence and a loving fear.
Take all thy part,
With lips as well as heart;
And posture keep; thy body 's surely more
Than beast dismounted at the church's door!

To sermon give attendance; note the text;
With ready mind,
Not critical inclined;
The bee did get no sweet,
Were she not diligent with wings and feet:
Be not, in church, with worldly cares perplexed;
Thy friend forget,
Though he be next thee set;
Restrain thine eyes that they not wander round,
And, cheerful, give the alms in duty bound;
One thing the more:
The ritual service o'er,
For prayer, in silence, heart and knee each bend,
That worship, so begun, so may it end.

ADVENT.

By L. S.

"HE comes!" Clear, through the stillness of the air,
    Rings the glad warning, "Lo, your King doth
    come!
Make straight His path to every heart and home,
Your thoughts make pure, for His approach prepare.

" Deck His bless'd house, with fragrant wreaths of pine,
With spruce and hemlock, and bright holly spray.
Your loving offerings on His altar lay!
Hail Him the Prince of Royal David's line!"

Like warrior, listening for commanding word,
Like virgin, who has watched, through the long night,
Guarding with care her taper's feeble light,
To open at the coming of her Lord,

The Church now rises at the welcome sound.
" He comes! He comes! Oh, joy! that I may meet
My Infant King, and worship at His feet.
Rejoice with me! The Master I have found!"

With hand upon the latchet of the door,
With ear attent to hear His hastening feet,
She waits and watches, for her joy complete;
" Until He come," repeating o'er and o'er.

ADVENT.

By Harriet Brewer.

THE whole world thrills expectant,
It waits a Presence sweet ;
The earth prepares her offering
To cast before His feet.

To greet the coming Christ-child
The oaks glow, far and wide ;
The heart-blood of the maples
Rises in crimson tide.

The birches bear gold for Him,
It gleams 'gainst pine trees dense ;
The air of Indian summer
Is faint with frankincense.

A quiet fills the forest,
The pines in whispers sing ;
In stillness loyal nature
Waits her returning King.

ADVENT.

By Abbie F. Judd.

WHY tarriest thou my Lord ?
The shadows deepen early,
And the chill snowflakes pearly
Come sadly fluttering earthward through the air;
The year grows old and weakens,
We see the distant beacons
Of the brave and young new year that shineth fair, —
Why tarriest thou, O Lord ?

Tarry no longer, Lord !
Our vision waxeth clearer
As Advent draweth nearer ;
And we wait Thy promised coming day by day ;
Help us to rightly meet Thee
With loving faith to greet Thee,
Lift up all bruised hearts along Thy way !
Tarry no longer, Lord !

Thou tarriest not, O Lord !
But comest with the dawning
Of the clear Christmas morning,
And in a manger makest Thy natal bed ;
Leaving the fair high places
To gladden earthly faces,
Thou bendest mightily Thy kingly Head,
And tarriest not, O Lord !

THE HERALDING.

By the Rev. Fred. C. Cowper.

YE little stars that shine above,
    Ye lamps illumining the night,
Ye sparkling splendors of God's love
    Dotting the spaces infinite —
        Whose path is in your keeping
        While weary worlds are sleeping,

Do angels pass with fluttering wing
    Adown your avenues of gold,
To bear a joyful heralding
    To aching hearts of baser mould,
        Who in the darkness dwelling
        Await the welcome telling ?

Yes ! to and fro they pass along
  Than the electric shafts more fleet,
More beautiful than minstrels' song
  Upon the mountains are their feet;
    Good tidings they are bringing
    More sweet than sweetest singing.

Theirs to proclaim Redemption's Day
  To sinners and to mortal men,
The day of Christ's imperial sway
  When peace and love shall dwell again,
    Where now are hate and warring
    And sin's unholy jarring.

Then, O ye blessed, golden lights
  That mark the highways of the King,
Shine bright upon those angel flights
  That down to earth the Gospel bring,
    A Saviour's birth proclaiming,
    The Serpent's kingdom maiming,
    The reign of Truth restoring,
    All nations Christ adoring.

WATCH !

By A. L. C.

YE know not when I shall come ;
  It may be in morning light
When the bright sun creeps in your chamber door
  Dispelling the shadows of night.
It may be in early morning,
  E'er the shadows have left the hills,
While yet the mist is rising
  From the pools and little rills.
I bid ye leave the door open,
  So the Spirit may come and go,
And tell me prepared you 're waiting
  For the hour that ye do not know.

Ye know not when I shall come :
   It may be in noon-day heat,
When home from the work of the harvest field
   You are turning with weary feet.
It may be as you sit talking,
   About the long days and your care,
That the first sweet notes of the Angels
   May be borne to you, through the air.
So I bid ye watch for my coming ;
   If the door is shut and fast,
I no longer can plead to enter ;
   I must turn from you at last.

Ye know not when I shall come :
   It may be when evening gray,
Is making long, black shadows,
   From the poplars over the way.
It may be when lamps are burning.
   As your little ones cluster round,
That faint in the far off heavens
   My coming to you may sound.
So, watch ! let the house be in order,
   Keep a guard about the door,
That I — thy Christ — may enter
   And abide forevermore.

Yea, Lord ! I 'll await Thy coming,
   Be it morning, noon, or night ;
I will list with the heart of a watcher
   Whose master may come in sight.
And the door will be always open
   For fear that I, in my sleep,
May wake too late to unlatch it
   When I hear Thy coming feet.
So I 'll wait for the time I know not
   When my waiting shall be done :
For I only know He bids me watch,
   And says, " I will surely come."

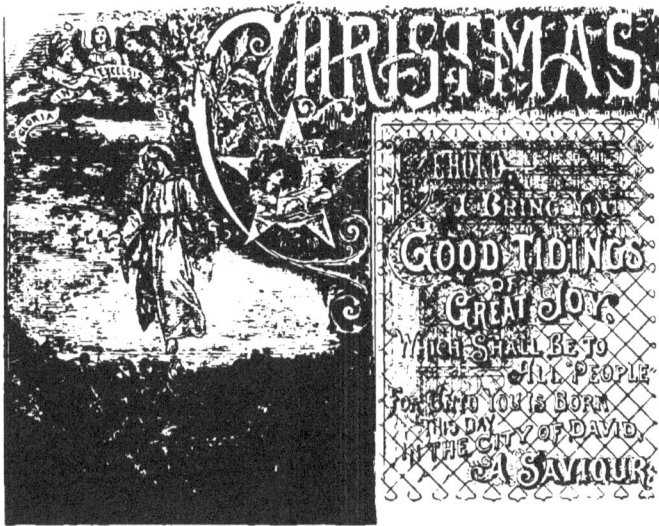

"PEACE ON EARTH."

By Maria Batterham Lindesey.

ACROSS the ages that have rolled
    Their tide on tide of dross and gold,
A message comes this Christmas-tide,
A message for the world so wide ;
        " Peace on Earth."

Peace to the breast that conflict fills
A wondrous peace that soothes and stills,
And all Life's beauty aye fulfils ;
        " Peace on Earth."

Peace to the heart that mourns its dead,
Shrinking the onward way to tread,
And scarcely daring to be led ;
        " Peace on Earth."

Peace to the soul that cannot soar,
Groping upon earth's darkened shore,
Peace and good will for evermore ;
        " Peace on Earth."

A CHRISTMAS CAROL.

By Marion Couthouy Smith.

TWELVE o'clock on Christmas Eve !
  Early Christmas bells are ringing,
Christians all, no longer grieve —
  Let your sighs be changed to singing !
Earth is dreaming, fair in seeming,
  Bathed in moonlight, wrapped in snow ;
Soft stars glisten while we listen
  To that song of long ago !

Long ago the heavens were thrilled
  With unearthly song and splendor,
While in helpless slumber stilled,
  Lay the Christ-child, pure and tender ;
Mary keeping, o'er His sleeping,
  Steadfast watch that mothers know,
Loving, wondering, mutely pondering,
  In the dark night, long ago.

Earth lay palled in silent gloom,
  Heeding not the heavenly numbers ;
He Who broke her ancient doom
  Roused her not from death-cold slumbers !
Two saints only, watching lonely,
  Three old sages, journeying slow,
Shepherds meeting gave their greeting,
  At the King's Birth, long ago.

Yet all heaven was moved to praise
  Him Who left her courts to save us :
And the whole world now shall raise
  Joy-songs for the Life He gave us !
Starry regions, angel legions,
  Realms of deepest dark below —
All were shaken, and o'ertaken
  By His glory, long ago.

Six o'clock on Christmas morn !
Hark ! the happy chimes are ringing!
Christians all, the Prince is born !
Come, your gifts of homage bringing.
Earth is waking, dawn scarce breaking,
Through the dark His altars glow ;
Here we meet in joyful greeting
Him who came so long ago !

A CHRISTMAS CARMEN.

By Mrs. S. A. Brock Putnam.

EVENING had trailed its purple shades
Across Judea's plain,
And silvery stars looked down from heaven
And glassed them in the main ;
When lo ! from out the dusky east,
Gleamed forth a meteor bright,
Which shone as shines no other star
That gems the brow of night.

Low hung it seemed, like friendly lamp,
Betwixt the sky and earth,
Without a sister of its kind,
A strange mysterious birth
Of soft, benignant radiance,
And lustre pure and clear ;
No fiery orb of menace dire
That shakes the soul with fear.

That star, in far off foreign land,
Three wise men, watching, saw, —
Three Magi, in Chaldea famed
In astrologic law ;

And straightway girding up their loins,
   With pleasure and amaze,
They, treasure-laden, followed swift
   The sure and steady blaze.

O'er hill and vale, through field and wood,
   It safely guided them,
Until it stood with broadening beams
   O'er little Bethlehem,
Above a stable, small and mean,
   Which entering they found
A mother with a smiling Babe —
   The wondering beasts around.

A manger was the cradle rude,
   And straw the Infant's bed ;
Yet shining glory filled the place
   And crowned the Infant's head.
Then, kneeling low, with reverent awe,
   They gave Him homage meet,
And laid their gold and frankincense
   And myrrh before His feet.

For well they knew this gracious Child
   Had come on earth to reign —
A King, a Priest, a mortal man,
   With all man's care and pain —
The promised Shiloh of His race ;
   Messias ! as foretold
In sacrifice and prophecy,
   Since Israel's days of old.

They left the Babe.   No more we know
   Of them, the favored three,
Who, guided by His natal star,
   The Saviour came to see.
But far beyond the nether realms
   That stud the arching sky,
Glad angels and archangels sang
   " Glory to God on high ! "

And still throughout the courts of heaven,
That joyous pæan rings :
" Glory to God, and peace on earth ! "
Each grateful seraph sings.
" Glory to God ! " our hearts respond :
And all our souls, aflame
With gratitude, and love, and praise,
Would sing Immanuel's name !

ONE CHRISTMAS EVE.

BY THE REV. HENRY G. PERRY.

THANKSGIVING had hardly come and gone,
When the children kept counting, one by one
The days until Christmas.   The night before,
A woe-begone woman was walking the floor,
And spoke to herself in a nervous tone :
" 'T was little we had for Thanksgiving, alas !
And now it is come to a sorry pass ;
There is n't much more than a crust and a bone
In the cupboard to-day — God help the poor !
And *me*, this Christmas, with children four.
There 's Ned, and Jim, and Prue, and Tim,
But I have n't a penny for one of them ;
Not even a capon, to make believe
We 've a turkey small !   So it goes, and I grieve
And fret, and drudge for our daily bread,
Till my heart seems sick and sore and dead."

The children, meanwhile, where were they all ?
Ned, and slim Jim, and Prue, and Tim small
Had been out to gather some sticks that day,
And coming back in their wonted way,
Crouched 'neath the window broken and old ;
There, in the gloaming, ill-clad and cold,

3

They o'erhear the plaint of their mother sad,
And said to each other, " It *is* too bad,"
As, hands all hold of the string to the sled,
They passed around silently into the shed.

" I say," said Ned, "it is *too* bad ! "   Said Prue,
" I say so too."   Said Jim, " But what 'll we do ? "
" Let us ask for our daily bread," said Tim small ;
" There 's none in the house, but our Father feeds all,
So now we 'll *ask*, since our dear father 's dead ;
When he was alive we never lacked bread.
How well I remember, before he died,
Reading the good Book one day by his side,
Where it told of the widow's and orphan's God :
' Don't forget that,' said he, ' when I 'm under the sod.'
And, I 'm *not* going to !   Let us ask of Him,
Just as we used to ask *father*," said Tim.
So down in a corner they knelt in the shed,
As Hope's hearty utterance heavenward sped.

Now Gruff, the green-grocer, was striding along
With Bovus the butcher, when outspoken, strong
From the shed came the words of the children's prayer;
The two men stopped short at each other to stare.
" Well, well ! " muttered Bovus.   " I vow ! " added Gruff.
" No noise — come away ; such a basket of stuff
As we 'll make up and leave 'em to-night
On the quiet !   That 's a very uncommon bright
Youngster, that Timmy !   Oh, did n't *he* pray
Though ? a reg'lar out-and-out Christmas-day
Trust-the-Lord sort of prayer !   We don't often hear
It clean-cut like that, eh, Bovus ?   It 's clear
To my mind that they are a good little lot,
And the youngest 's a fam'ly forget-me-not."

And off through the dark the two men stole,
While Tim to his mother ran in, and told
Of a curious noise they heard in the shed
Just after the prayer for their daily bread.

But she answered him never a word
When he asked her, did n't she think it the Lord? —
Only sung an odd bit of a sad old tune,
And said, " 'T will be children's bed-time soon.
Put a few fresh branches, dear, on the fire,
And I 'll tell you a story before we retire.

" There once was a King — "   " What kind? " said Tim
         small.
" King of Kings, they called Him, because for all
He came, as our Prophet, Priest, and King,
Peace on earth and good-will, Christ was born to bring.
And so sang angels at time of his birth,
' Good-will to men, and Peace on earth ! '
After all, children dear, Oh, never forget
How angels may minister to us yet.
Though the night be dark, so sure as the bright
Light of day break, it will all come *right !* "

And just as the widow said " *right,*" back
Echoed the word from the door; while — Thwack ! —
Whack !! Smack ! ! ! three singular thumps on the floor
Of the stoop outside — and they heard no more.
" It 's the angel ! " said Tim, with a wary crook
Of his neck about. " Just let 's take a look,
If no one 's afraid ! "   And out with a bound
He went, and what d'ye think he found?
An enormous hamper, that to pull in, Prue
Ned, Jim, and Tim had all they could do.

A turkey that weighed twenty pounds if an ounce,
And parcels of goodies that made small Tim bounce
Up and down, till at last he fell over flat
And trod on the tail of the thin tabby cat,
And then a huge ham, with celery too;
Bread, butter, and oysters enough for a stew;
Parsnips, potatoes, cranberries, cheese,
Crackers, sugar, tea, coffee —   Please
Excuse naming all the family found had
Been packed in that hamper to make them glad.

And, rest assured, ere sleep shut their eyes,
From the humble cot to the Lord of the skies
And earth — great Giver of every good —
Mother and children gave thanks for the food
Besought not in vain.   Love prompted the deed,
And kindness responded to urgent need.
Ah ! little ones all, let your hearts be true
To do unto others as you 'd have *them* do
To you!   And ye parents, remember the " Rule,"
And while you train them, keep *yourselves* in that school.

ON CHRISTMAS ALL HOLY.

By L. D. C.

OH, what shall we sing
    To Christ Jesus our King
On Christmas all holy?
His praises we 'll sing ;
Through the sky let them ring
From hearts meek and lowly.

What shall we present
To hail His descent
On Christmas all holy?
Adoration present
And truly repent
With hearts meek and lowly.

Pure gold we will bring,
Fit gift for a King,
On Christmas all holy :
True love we will bring,
The best offering,
From hearts meek and lowly :

Frankincense for the Priest
Who from sin hath released,
On Christmas all holy,
Our souls. O High Priest,
At Thy heavenly Feast
Grant hearts meek and lowly !

Self-sacrifice give,
And others forgive,
On Christmas all holy:
This the myrrh we will give
To Him who doth live
In hearts meek and lowly.

If thus of our treasure
We give without measure
On Christmas all holy,
Kingly Babe, our soul's Treasure,
Thou wilt dwell — wondrous pleasure ! —
In hearts meek and lowly.

DEAR OLD SANTA CLAUS.

By F. Burge Griswold.

" DEAR Old Santa Claus ! How do you do?
I have been looking this twelve-month for you.
Never has time seemed so weary and slow
As since the last Christmas, a year ago.
Where have you been, sir ? What under the sun
Have you been thinking, and what have you done?
So many children to welcome your face !
So many longing to meet your embrace !
Surely you should n't have tarried away :
Rather let Christmas-time come every day."

Santa Claus shook off the snow from his back,
Loosed and put down his cumbersome pack,

Threw his fur robes and his gloves on a chair,
Took his seal cap from his thick, grizzled hair,
Laughed long and loud at the sweet little girl,
Wound on his finger a soft, golden curl,
Gave her a kiss on her fair, dimpled cheek,
Then, with a nod, condescended to speak.

" My little maid, I am right glad to come,
Bringing good cheer to yourself and your home.
I 've been as busy as busy could be
All the long time since you parted from me.
Such a wide journey all over the world,
By the swift speed of my reindeers whirled!
Now in the valley, and then up so high
You would have thought I could reach to the sky.
Sometimes I stopped to buy beautiful things, —
Candies and toys, silver thimbles, gold rings,
Dollies and trinkets, and books rich and rare,
Such as would suit my young friends everywhere.
Fitting selection is no easy task ;
But to give pleasure is all that I ask, —
Only to see the dear boys and girls glad
Fully repays all the labor I 've had.
I 've been as eager as you could well be
For the blessed night with the bright Christmas-tree,
And the old open chimneys, with little sabots
Placed in the corners, and tiniest hose
Hung from the mantels, awaiting my sleigh,
At every benevolent visit I pay.
Now it is here, I must up and be doing ;
Other sweet children are worthy the wooing.
As to your parcels, to-morrow will show :
You 'll find your red stocking filled up from the toe."

Was it a dream?   When the clear morning broke,
Early the dear little maiden awoke,
        Snow-birds were twittering,
        Icicles glittering,
Diamonds and pearls making brilliant the scene:

Merry bells ringing,
Gay carols singing,
Everywhere garlands of fresh evergreen ;
Hearts beat so merrily,
Things went so cheerily,
Harp and dulcimer all the day long.
Up from the pillow white
Sprang my sweet little sprite,
Clasping her hands as she looked o'er the scene ;
Unto faith's listening ear
Angel songs were so clear
Almost she thought to see bright forms on high.
Eager, yet soft and low,
Whispered she, " Oh, I know !
This is the Christmas Day.   Santa Claus dear,
While I was sleeping
Came slyly peeping
Into my room to see if I were here.
What has he left for me ?
I will soon run and see.
First let me thank the good Lord for His love, —
It would be sad indeed
If for an earthly greed
I could forget the great Gift from above."

Down by her nest of snow
Knelt she, with face aglow,
Speaking as if to a visible friend : —
" Father, I think of Thee
Gladly and gratefully
For all the good it has pleased Thee to send.
But there is one best thing
Christmas must always bring,
And only one :
By Thy most precious grace
Make my heart fitting place
For Thy dear Son.
May I be meek and mild,
Like to the Holy Child ;
Let Him be always here in my sweet home.

If He will dwell with me,
All will be well with me;
Where the dear Jesus is no ill can come."

Who saw the wings of gold
Flutter, and gently fold
Round that dear object of God's tender care?
Up in the heavenly place
" Their angels " see the face
Of the great Father of faith and of prayer.
Blessed are those that know
Such ministry below!
Blessed the heart of an innocent child!
In all humility
So must we learn to be
Like unto this little one undefiled.
Then shall the Christmas-tide
Blessing and joy abide,
There will be holy-day throughout the year;
All of this life will be
Foretaste of purity. —
Such as is known in the glorified sphere.

HAIL! HOLY SON OF GOD.

By the Rev. Arthur W. Little.

HAIL! Holy Son of God,
By whom the worlds were made;
To Thee, Eternal Word,
Angels their homage paid.
Wilt Thou in pitying love,
Ransom us from the grave,
Stoop from Thy throne above,
Mighty to save?

Hail! Son of maiden mild,
Whom prophets did foretell;
God, as a little child,
Comes down with us to dwell.
Angels, to Bethlehem fly;
Sing ye Messiah's birth:
Glory to God on High,
 And peace on earth.

Hail! God Incarnate born;
Angels still worship Thee;
Shepherds, ere break of dawn,
Hasten their Lord to see.
Lo! from the Orient far
Wise men their offerings bring,
Led by Thy natal star,
 Own Thee their King.

Jesus, our Saviour dear,
We, too, would worship Thee,
Joining with angels here
In heavenly minstrelsy.
Thy love doth never fail;
Shall we not love Thee well?
Hail! Mary's Son, all hail!
 Immanuel.

CRADLE HYMN OF THE VIRGIN.

By Abbie F. Judd.

" DORMI Jesu, mater ridet,
 Quæ tam dulcem somnum videt,
Dormi Jesu blandule;
Si non dormis, mater plorat,
Inter fila cantans orat,
 Blande, veni, somnule."

"Sleep, my Jesu, tenderly!"
    Sang a mother long ago,
'Neath the soft Judean starlight,
Keeping watch into the far night,
    Crooning lovingly and low,
"Sleep, my Jesu, tenderly!"

"Come, soft slumber, balmily,
    Kiss his eyelids soft and fair,"
Sang the mother, while adoring
Angels joined the chorus, soaring,
    In strange melody and rare —
"Come, soft slumber, balmily!"

"If thou sleep not, mother mourns,"
    Sang the virgin meek and mild,
Clasping close, with pure affection,
To her bosom's sure protection,
    Jesus Christ, her little child —
"If thou sleep not, mother mourns."

"Sleep, my Jesu, tenderly!
    Take thy rest and fear no ill,
Mother's arms shall safe enfold thee,
While the wond'ring kings behold thee,
    And with gifts thy cradle fill.
Sleep, my Jesu, tenderly!"

GLORY BE TO GOD ON HIGH.

By J. J. L. ENGLAND.

SING the mystery of Love,
    Tell the wonder of this morn,
Sing with angel hosts above,
    Christ the Prince of Peace is born!

Sing the song that shepherds heard,
Catch the heavenly strain again,
Sing of Christ, Incarnate Word,
Peace on earth, good will to men!

Sing, ye wandering orbs of light,
Blazing in the heavens afar,
Lo! from out the shades of night,
Shines the bright and Morning Star!

Mortals join the choirs above,
On this happy Christmas morn,
Sing the mystery of love,
Unto us a Child is born!

All creation join and sing,
  Swell the chorus of the sky,
Glory to the New Born King!
Glory be to God on High!

BIRTH-SONG OF THE MESSIAH.

By William B. Chisholm.

I hear the voices of sweet seraphim
  Tuning the natal hymn;
And shepherds resting on the star-lit plain
Catch up the glad refrain.

Wild is the wind on lone Judean steep
That cradles Nature's sleep;
Yet winds shall hush in gentlest lullaby
The Infant Christ-Child's cry.

Bring richest gifts! ye wanderers of the East,
To deck the royal feast;
Bend low, ye kings, and girdled warriors bow
Before your Monarch now!

Oh! deck the shrine of holy praise and prayer
With all that is most fair
Of floral garniture, and loudly ring
Your welcome to the King!

Beneath the green and star-bespangled arches,
A joyous army marches,
Of the young Child's own chosen little ones,
Wafting their antiphons.

Sing to new-born Messiah songs most sweet,
Here in His temple meet
For His blest feast; from garners full outpour
Harvest and vintage store.

What though skies scowl, and o'er earth's snowy breast
The nightly shadows rest;
There is no night in this glad feast of souls.
Hark, how the anthem rolls !

" All glory be to God enthroned on high ;
  To mortals, peace and love ;
Look down, Thou blest Immanuel, look down,
  With favor from above ! "

A CHRISTMAS EVERGREEN.

By Maie Allyne.

'TWAS the merry Christmas eve, and gay
    Were the streets of that great city's heart
With hastening ones, and rich display
  Of beauteous gifts that friends impart.

There were faces kind, and faces bright
  Of rich and poor, of old and young,
There were those who walked in God's pure light,
  There were starving ones that throng among.

And looking down through ether blue
  Were angels who had sung His birth,
To see what the moving throng would do
  For the Holy Child who walked the earth.

They saw, in a widow's cheerless room,
  Two little ones with fever burned,
Whose love had brightened the way of gloom ;
  There, one in the art of healing learned

Had found them, radiant, though forlorn ;
  For the mother's love had placed between,
In memory of the Christ-Child born,
  A poor little waif of evergreen.

Two mottoes hung from the slender tree,
And the light of tapers two burned there,
While the sick were pillowed restfully;
A picture sweet in the room so bare.

The story he told when lights burned low,
Where three little stockings brimming held
Such pretty toys; with the morning's glow,
His generous children, love impelled,

Sent gifts, which the two might waking find,
Whose faces bright he had seen that eve,
And the giving made their hearts more kind,
For the thread of joy small hands could weave.

Ring merrily out, ye Christmas chimes!
For gracious years of the story old.
Sing His gentle words, these festal times,
Whose love, in charity sweet, is told.

THE NATIVITY.

By the Rev. F. W. Taylor, S. T. D.

IN humble guise, an Infant fair
    Thou cam'st, our human form to wear,
        O Son of God Most High!
In darkest night Thy beaming Star
Shed o'er the nations near and far
        The light of heaven brought nigh.

As in Thy Blessed Mother's care
Thou gently sleepest, earth's keen air
        Trembles with angel songs.
"Peace on the earth! To men good will!
Glory to God!" and "Glory!" still
        The heavenly choir prolongs.

In mystic vision, round Thy stall
Behold great kings and prophets, all
    Of Israel's sacred line;
While seers of Gentile race proclaim
The world's desire in Thy sweet name,
    And hail Thee Son Divine.

SAINT STEPHEN'S DAY.

BY MARION COUTHOUY SMITH.

WHO art thou, Warrior, bright and bold,
    With armor of silver and crown of gold?
— The soldier of Jesus Christ am I,
First of His host that went forth to die.

What are those palms that o'er thee wave?
— The sign of my victory over the grave.
Who gave thee power to conquer so?
— Jesus Christ on His Cross of woe.

Why is thy face as calm and bright
As an angel's standing in God's own sight?
— I saw the light of His eyes and brow;
My face, as a mirror, reflects it now.

What are those stains on thine armor spread?
— The blood that for His dear sake I shed.
What is that trophy thou bear'st in hand?
— The stone that slew me at His command.

What is that ring, as of sunbeams bright,
That circles thy brow with wondrous light?
— God opened Heaven, and His rays came down —
About my head, like a shining crown.

What are those words, so strangely sweet,
That ever thy smiling lips repeat?
— I prayed, "Forgive them!" and He for this,
Taught me His sweetest song of bliss.

Why dost thou beckon and call me so?
I fear to follow thy path of woe!
— Never fear! In the ways of pain,
They who follow find richest gain.

What is the joy that with thee they share,
The badge of the Crucified who wear?
— No words can tell it — no heart hath known
The endless joy that He gives His own!

How shall I win it, O warrior bright?
— Wait on His will by day and night;
Bear all for Him, and like Him forgive,
So with Him shalt thou die — and live!

ST. STEPHEN.

By Isabel G. Eaton.

HE stands the first of those the Master willed
    Should wear the Martyr's crown,
First of the glorious ones whose blood was spilled,
    Through all the ages down.
His youthful feet pressed on that mystic way,
The royal road of human agony,
    Nor feared he shout nor frown.

Thou with the angel-face! Transfigured ere
    The spirit left its clay,
What heavenly voice commands thy listening ear
    That thou the call obey?
It is the Lord! The heavens opened wide,
Thy mortal eyes the sinless One descried,
    Beckoning thy soul away.

Not long thy toiling in the Master's field,
    Not long the race to run,

4
.

Though wondrous fruits thy tireless labors yield
    From rise till set of sun.
O eager soul! with zealous love aflame
To teach the world the power of Jesus' Name,
    Too soon thy victory won.

But though thy hands shall never celebrate
    The Sacrifice divine,
Offered by those who at His altar wait —
    The mystic Bread and Wine —
No Sacrament thy soul immortal needs,
On Jesus glorified thy spirit feeds,
    The Church Triumphant thine!

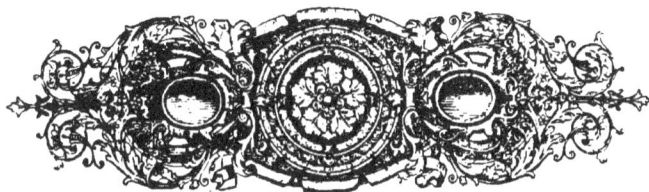

THE INNOCENTS' DAY.

By the Rev. C. W. Leffingwell, D.D.

THE merry Christmas bells have ceased to ring
 Their Alleluiahs at the Saviour's birth;
The happy choirs are still, they cannot sing
 To-day their song of joy in heaven and earth.

The manger-cradle is forsaken now;
 Not even there, the Saviour's head may rest.
Thorn-crowned already is that placid brow;
 The sword, even now, doth pierce the mother's breast.

Her Child shall live to bear the cruel cross,
 But all the babes in Bethlehem are dead.
Poor Rachel mourns, and knows not, in her loss,
 How Christian mothers may be comforted.

They know, as she knew not, the gracious end
 In all these dealings of the blessed Lord, —
How in His tender mercy He doth lend
 These little ones to witness for His word.

To Him alone all years of life belong;
 He knoweth when to give and take away;
For His high purpose weakness is made strong,
 A thousand years are counted as a day.

All life and death His providence fulfil, —
 The days of childhood and the years of man;
No life so short that doth not do His will,
 No death so early as to fail His plan.

The Holy Innocents of Bethlehem,
And all sweet children that have ever died
Are safe with Him; no harm can come to them,
No one can take them from the Saviour's side.

Though absent, still, O Rachel! they are thine;
Such earthly loss, in Paradise is gain.
Set full with stars, in Heaven their crowns shall shine —
Their little lives have not been lived in vain.

Then keep with chastened joy the children's day!
O mourner! see, by faith, the happy throng
Around the Lamb, there evermore to stay
And sing before the throne the blest new song.

THE HOLY INNOCENTS.

By Isabel G. Eaton.

" Not in speaking, but in dying, have they confessed Christ."

SWEET flower-faces! seen through fronds of palm,
  Whose golden aureole
Reflects a light born of no earthly charm,
  Given each infant soul.

Slain for the Christ-child whom they never knew,
  Have they the story learned?
For His eternal glory, children too
  The martyr's crown have earned.

Haste, little ones, the risen Christ to meet,
  Who bade your souls go free!
Go follow in His train, and kiss His feet, —
  Your eyes shall opened be,

To see immortal visions, fairer far
　　Than given to earthly eyes;
Your souls be pearls of Heaven — each a star.
　　To shine in Paradise.

Sweet Innocents !   The holy angels learn
　　With you this mystery;
How Love Divine could from His Kingdom turn,
　　And God Incarnate be.

In golden carols He your lips has blessed,
　　To mortal speech denied;
In speaking not, in dying ye confessed
　　The Christ once crucified.

Lead, little feet, our own to wander through
　　The streets of Paradise !
Through mists the stars shine dim — but to our view
　　The hills of heaven arise.

Our hearts are faint, our steps are slow — but He
　　Who called the children home
Pleads that the Vision Blest our souls may see.
　　O come, Lord Jesu ! come !

NEW YEAR'S EVE.

By the Rev. C. W. Leffingwell, D.D.

THE night is starry, bright, and clear,
  With moonlight glimmering on the snow ;
  And midnight winds, with voices low,
Sing dirges for the dying year.

How strangely beautiful the night!
  And yet to some, alas, how sad ! —
  Whose hearts, last New Year gay and glad,
Are now bereft of hope and light.

Unwelcome too to him, in truth,
  Whose tyrant memory will not sleep,
  But brings back from oblivion's deep
Each folly of his wasted youth ;

Reminds him of the golden days
  That have departed, one by one, —
  The little good his life has done,
And all the error of his ways.

But hark ! The bell strikes twelve o'clock :
  A year has passed, to come no more ;
  And as we listen, at the door
We seem to hear a stranger knock.

Old Year, I pray we part as friends !
  Sincerely we can say " Adieu ! "
  And as we welcome in the New
We promise him to make amends, —

We pledge ourselves to nobler deeds,
  To loftier thought, and purer life,
  To be more faithful in the strife
For what our nobler nature pleads.

Remembering all the solemn past,
  Its lessons treasured in the heart,
  So we will live and act our part
As if this New Year were our last.

THE OLD AND THE NEW.

By Callie L. Bonney.

AT portal of the heavenly land,
  Where beauteous pearl gates gleaming stand,
    The Old Year waits,
His earthly work and mission done,
To yield his regal crown to one
    Beyond the gates.

His silver hair in fading light
Has caught the gleam of sunset bright, —
    A halo fair, —
It touches with majestic grace
The noble beauty of his face,
    And lingers there.

His aged hands a volume hold
Where story of his reign is told,
    Its loss and gain, —
Some spotless pages, writ in gold ;
While others legends dark unfold
    Of wrong and pain.

But joyous bells proclaim at last
The Old Year's reign is of the past ;
And open gates
Admit to earth a youthful King,
While golden chimes exultant ring
And Hope awaits.

THE OLD YEAR.

By F. R. W.

Here we have no continuing city. — Hebrews xiii. 14.

OH that the pilgrim years would sometimes stay ! —
  Stay for a little where the palm-trees bend,
And with the willows in the trembling stream
    Their shadows blend !
Alas ! they may not stay ; for through the sandy plain
And rocky vale life's journey must be pressed
    To its true rest.

But as we leave behind our happy days,
Though thought of change may bring the rising tear,
Yet to the future dim we turn our face,
    And feel no fear ;
For He who through the burning desert guides
Knows when the weary feet need healing balm
    And nights of calm.

No fear that little ones with tender limbs
Should be o'erdriven by the Love that leads ;
Labor and rest are set by One who knows
    All our hearts' needs ;
And while our tents are struck or pitched again
At eve, alike, O Lord, our souls can rest
    On Thy dear breast.

THE EPIPHANY.

By N. M. Hitchcock.

THE Christmas carols die away, —
   The strains of holy mirth
With which that blessed natal day
   Is hymned by heaven and earth;
The Church in triumph now doth sing
That Bethlehem's babe is Christ the King;
And, while the Magi bend the knee,
She hails his glad EPIPHANY !

Once over trackless realms of night
   The voice of God was heard, —
The voice that said, " Let there be light !"
   And light sprang at the word.

The morning stars then sang for joy ;
A nobler theme is our employ
When, Light of Lights, we bow to Thee,
Hailing Thy blest EPIPHANY !

Streaming with dazzling beams from heaven,
    Shineth the light of day,
White with prismatic colors seven
    Mingling in one pure ray :
Thus with the " seven-fold gifts " divine
The Sun of Righteousness doth shine ;
And as His glorious beams we see
We hail His bright EPIPHANY !

And, kneeling at His feet, implore
    Our path may be the way
That shineth ever more and more
    Unto the perfect day ;
'Till in the heavenly city bright,
That needs of sun nor moon the light,
We, in His likeness clothed, may be
Blest in that great EPIPHANY !

THE FEAST OF CANDLEMAS.

BY W. B. CHISHOLM.

WITH burnished lamps and bright
    In dim midwinter light
Let altars gleam, and for thy festal theme
The Christ-Child in the temple : there behold
Long waiting Simeon, — seer and holy sage,
Last relic of the old Hebraic age ;
Rejoicing he to welcome this the Child
Whose star of late made glad the winter mild.

The sheaves of glad ingathering
  Are withered now,
And the tiny buds of nearing spring
  Shiver beneath pathless snow.
O soul, hast thou no flowers
To glad these holy hours?
No garden, thou my heart,
Warmed by thy pious art,
Screened from the north-wind's breath?
Is it winter all, and death?
Shall not sweet Candlemas be gay
With rose or marigold, I pray,
Wreathen with green of Yule?
There in the frozen pool
Methought the lily raised its head
From its ice-tomb, pale and dead,
If it might but honored be,
Culled and laid on the altar there,
While the sweet strains of festivity
Gladden the morn's chill air,
And the lamps of Candlemas grow bright
O'er the dark midwinter night.

LENTEN TWILIGHT.

BY THE REV. C. W. LEFFINGWELL, D. D.

THROUGH the twilight into darkness,
 Daylight glories gently fade,
And by exquisite gradations
 Sunlight passes into shade;
Ever between light and shadow
 Some soft middle-tint is laid.

As in all the world around us,
 So through all the world within;
Daylight joys in twilight linger
 When our nights of grief begin;
Over sadness broods the memory
 Of the gladness that has been.

In the Church, by such transition,
 Changes now the Christian year;
And between the light and shadow
 Mellow middle-tints appear —
God's great love and glory blending
 With our night of evil here.

Ere the Lenten shadows deepen,
 While before our dazzled eyes
Fades Epiphany's great splendor,
 Blessed twilight veils the skies,
And the star of Bethlehem lingers
 Over where the young Child lies.

SEPTUAGESIMA.

By Thomas Mair.

THE Christmas garlands withered lie
    Upon the frozen earth,
Type of the soon forgotten vows
    We made at Jesus' birth.

The rosy flush of early morn
    Has changed to noontide's ray,
As life's first hopes and joys depart,
    When trials crowd its day.

The guiding star no longer leads
    The pilgrim's onward way,
Through gloom and desert to the place
    Where once the Saviour lay.

But Lord, Thy weary feet once trod
    The path our feet must tread,
And Thou hast felt the pain and grief
    Which bow each drooping head.

To Thee alone we look for aid,
    Though love seems faint and chill,
For Thou hast felt the tempter's power
    And foiled his work of ill.

We ask not that Thy loving care
    Bid earthly sorrow flee;
For pain and anguish, by Thy grace,
    Bring contrite hearts to Thee.

We only pray that Thou wilt make
    Our souls, by worldly loss,
More like to Thine, that we may share,
    The blessings of Thy Cross.

QUINQUAGESIMA.

By N. M. Hitchcock.

THE Church doth many lessons teach
  Of faith, and hope, and love.
She bids us learn their blessedness
  And all their sweetness prove,
As through the " Christian zodiac "
  The hallowed seasons move.

Now as the Lenten warning sounds,
  She calls to fast and prayer,
That all our works are nothing worth
  Unless that love we share, —
The love that led the sinless One
  For man the cross to bear.

She bids us learn the charity
  That seeketh not its own;
She telleth us how mighty love
  Did for our sins atone,
And how our Elder Brother bore
  For us the cross alone.

Her voice we heed, and pray Thee, Lord.
  For the perfect charity,
Without which, whosoever lives
  Is counted dead by Thee —
That gift of gifts, which greater is
  Than to know all mystery.

Knowledge shall fail and pass away,
  The gift of tongues shall cease;
But charity remains for aye,
  The very bond of peace;
Oh! send Thy Holy Spirit, Lord;
  Our charity increase!

So shall we keep the " Feast of feasts,"
With hearts from self set free;
So shall we dwell in perfect love, —
   Thy children's liberty;
So shall we hear the Master say,
" Ye blessed, come to me ! "

FAITH, HOPE, AND LOVE.

By Mary Ann Thomson.

FOR Faith that conquers earth;
   For Hope, our anchor sure ;
For Love, of heavenly birth,
   That, fadeless, shall endure ;
Let praise ascend to God above,
   Giver of Faith and Hope and Love.

By faith we look on God
   By mortal eye unseen ;
We mark His guiding rod,
   And on His staff we lean ;
The banner of the cross unfurled
We grasp, and overcome the world.

By hope our spirits soar
   To join the victor band,
Who on the blissful shore
   With crowns and palms shall stand.
Like ships that safely anchored lie,
Are hearts whose hope is set on high.

By love our souls we yield
   To God, who deigns to call;
And strive that all be healed
   By Him who died for all ;
Faith, hope, and love our hearts uplift,
But love, we own, the greatest gift.

Faith shall give place to sight
  When earth shall pass way
And hope, to sweet delight.
  When dawns eternal day;
But love refined, where all is pure
To endless ages shall endure.

A LENTEN LYRIC.

BY CATHARINE MARIA MORRIS.

AMID the shadows let me lie
   Where Thou didst agonize and die,
While my soul lifts its mournful cry!
          Mea culpa!

Of all Thy human nature bore,
The tempest's rush, the billows' roar,
The wandering feet from sea to shore.
          Mea culpa!

Faint by the wild Tiberian sea,
All spent and worn by Galilee.
Mighty to save, we cry to Thee,
          Mea culpa!

No plea have I from guilt and sin,
No claim the heavenly home to win,
Only Thy pardoning " Enter in."
          Mea culpa!

Above the cross. above the tomb.
Through all the Lenten shadow's gloom,
Doth light ineffable illume !
          Mea culpa!

LENT.

By Frances A. M. Johnson.

KNOW ye the Shepherd's voice? He calleth thee
  To leave the highways and the busy throng
On wealth and pleasure bent, to climb the steeps
Of sacrifice and chant the Lenten song.

He calleth thee to mountain solitudes
Where the world is not, but He its Saviour is ;
There to thy peaceful soul he will reveal
Himself and His most holy mysteries.

As to the world will He not speak to thee ;
Thou shalt behold His face, transfigured, shine,
And heaven descend upon the mountain's brow
Enfolding thee in clouds of light divine.

And if in duty's path thou find'st delight
In fond obedience to His gentle call,
Thou 'lt meet Him somewhere every day ; thy home,
A Bethany, will know His footsteps' fall.

If thou give but a cup of water cool
To do Him service, by the shady well
Thou 'lt find him resting when thou com'st to draw,
And in thy heart shall living waters swell.

And when the paschal moon at midnight moves
Above the olives of Gethsemane,
Tracing thy shadow and thy Saviour's on
The sward His feet pressed in His agony;

While Kedron murmurs o'er its stony bed,
He 'll tell thee all the wonders of that night
When Love Divine did sweat great drops of blood,
And angels strengthened Him for Calvary's height.

LENT.

By Thomas Mair.

AS the soft gleams at daylight's gentle close
　　With ling'ring beauty fill the scene with peace;
When the low murmurs of the woodland cease,
And every care is soothed to sweet repose
That life in fervid noontide never knows, —
So com'st thou, Lent, to bring my soul release
From thrall of sin ; to cleanse the soiled fleece
Of Christ's own flock in that pure stream which flows
Forever living from His riven side.
We rest beneath the shadow of the cross
Where once He hung, and though the world counts loss
Glad joys resigned, if we with Christ may bide
And share His sorrow, all the rest is dross,
For we shall gain the life for which He died.

A LENTEN HYMN.

By Mrs. J. L. Moore.

HEAR Thy servant's meditations, Lord of light and
　　love divine ! —
Hear my sad soul's supplications, and incline my will to
　　Thine !
I have suffered long and sadly, and my soul in darkness
　　pines ;
But to Thee I turn, oh, gladly ! — on Thy truth my heart
　　reclines.
May this time of prayer and fasting, all these hours of
　　holy rest,
Bring me treasures everlasting, be to me a season blest.

Purge my heart, O Lord, and try me, but with mercy's
    gentlest touch !
No good thing of Thine deny me! Let me love Thee
    overmuch !
Thou canst see my pride and passion, all my faults and
    follies view ;
Thou canst with divine compassion see my faults, and
    pity too.
Thou alone canst give me pardon, Thou alone affliction
    stay :
Take from me, most blessed Warden, sin and suffering
    away !
Fit me for the heavenly mansion, where alone is perfect
    peace, —
Where the soul, with sweet expansion, shall in godliness
    increase ;
And at last, when life is over, and this weary spirit free,
Take me, Jesus, Friend, and Lover, — take me home to
    dwell with Thee !

VIA DOLOROSA.

By Brad Courtland.

" ECCE HOMO !" said the Roman prelate Pilate,
    stern and loud ;
Answered back with fierce revilings the hard-hearted
    Jewish crowd ;
Came then from the grand Prætorium, with head thorn-
    crowned and bowed,
The Royal Victim stately, and behold, a pallid cloud
Shadowed Via Dolorosa, as the Roman prelate proud
Washed his hands before the rabble, and in trumpet
    tones and loud
Said the ban on every Jewish child and parent in the
    crowd.

The Royal Victim, bending underneath His weight of
 woe,
Climbed the Via Dolorosa eighteen hundred years ago, —
Left behind the glorious city bathed in richest Syrian
 glow,
While the branching limes and olives, swaying gently to
 and fro,
Kissed the heated brow of Him whose faltering steps and
 slow
Climbed up Via Dolorosa, fainting 'neath that weight of
 woe,
Jeered by the Jewish rabble eighteen hundred years ago.

Let us veil our Christian faces, we the Christians of
 to-day !
"Crucify Him, Crucify Him," did the Jewish rabble say !
Does no other heartless rabble catch the note from far
 away,
As it comes down through the ages of the dimming centuries gray ?
Lo ! the warm Egyptian lilies, blooming now as bloomed
 for aye ;
And the mellow Syrian sunset gathering jewels from the
 day !
Hear again the wandering echoes, "Crucify Him," do
 they say !

Floating down the tide of ages comes again the muffled
 strain —
"Crucify Him, Crucify Him ! on our children be the
 stain."
Drooped the gorgeous Syrian lilies, nestling in the golden
 grain —
On the Via Dolorosa did the Kingly Victim drain
All that bitter cup of anguish ; still the solemn, sad
 refrain
Is sent back through all the ages, "He is crucified again."
And alike on Jew and Gentile rests the seal of His blood
 stain.

A SONG FOR LENT.

By Flora L. Stanfield.

THE happiest time? If my halting rhyme
  Should herald the happiest days
That ever appear in the Christian's year
  And call us the Lord to praise,
It would turn to a song, with a purpose strong,
  To honor this season sweet
When we meet with Him in the dawning dim
  And kneel at His sacred feet.

The loveliest hue? It is neither the blue
  That lives in the cloudless sky,
Nor the blush which glows on the face of the rose
  As the sunbeam passes by ;
But the royal tint that its kisses print
  On the cheeks of the passion-flower, —
The violet sheen that is fitly seen
  At the Lenten trysting hour.

The sweetest tale? Let the thoughtless rail
  At the joy which the sick soul finds,
As the story old of the Cross is told
  And the Lenten scroll unwinds.
But we rejoice, as the preacher's voice
  Grows faint with the hallowed theme,
To think that we may his hearers be
  And the Lord's own servants seem.

And so we tread, divinely led,
  In the path that His patience tried,
And we share His fast that we may at last
  With Him at His feast abide.
We do not mourn for the garments torn
  In the fray with the scoffing world,
As we walk each day where he leads the way,
  With our violet flag unfurled.

LENT.

By L. D. S.

WITH whispered pleadings, soft and low, again
   The Saviour speaks in every heart and home, —
" I go to bear my cross in bitter pain :
   Wilt thou not, too, take up thy cross, and come?

" Thou didst my praises at the Christmas feast
   With happy heart continually sing ;
Thou wentest with the wise men of the East
   To my poor cradle costly gifts to bring.

" Would'st thou still wear the crown, yet bear no loss?
   Smile when I smile, yet never with me weep?
Would'st thou enjoy all gain, yet feel no loss ?
   Through all my agony for thee, still sleep?

" Oh ! if I left a heaven of perfect bliss,
   That thou mightest some day have it for thy home,
Wilt thou not do so small a thing as this,
   And when I call, take up thy cross and come? "

"GOOD LORD, DELIVER US."

By C. J. G.

FROM all the toils of evil men,
   From words unkind and hearts untrue,
From secret griefs which may have been,
   From cherished guilt of every hue —
      Deliver us, good Lord,
      According to Thy word.

From all the leprosy of sin, —
 That inward fretting. deep and dread,
That loathsome plague which spreads within,
 And living, counts us with the dead —
  Deliver us, good Lord.

From wandering feet which slip and slide
 Far from the blessed paths of peace,
From every ill which may betide,
 From all that stays our soul's increase —
  Deliver us, good Lord.

From all assaults of death and hell,
 All base allegiance with the foe —
Beguilings which we see full well,
 And subtle snares we may not know, —
  Deliver us, good Lord.

From all half-hearted fealty,
 Oh ! gracious Father, Helper, Friend,
From all ingratitude to Thee,
 Who lovest Thine own unto the end —
  Deliver us, good Lord.

By Thy divine and perfect grace,
 The love which makes us one with God,
By the compassion in Thy face ;
  Deliver us, good Lord.

By all the lame Thy hand hath healed,
 By all the suffering ones restored,
By all the blinded eyes unsealed;
  Deliver us, good Lord.

By every precious drop of blood
 For our redemption once outpoured,
By every hour on shameful rood —
  Deliver us, good Lord.

By every throb of mortal pain,
  By every trembling nerve and cord,
By all Thy loss — our dearest gain —
    Deliver us, good Lord.

Since Thou for us didst deign to die,
  O Son of Mary, Son of God !
Then by Thy last expiring cry —
    Deliver us, good Lord,
      According to Thy word.

THE SHADOW OF THE CROSS.

BY AMELIA TRUESDELL.

I SAW a peasant woman bent and old,
  With dusty footsteps tread the broad highway;
A burden on her patient shoulders lay;
Her brow bore trace of sorrows manifold.

I saw where one — perhaps for sins untold —
Had raised a wayside cross of massive stone;
Beneath its shadow where a fountain shone
She rested on the cool and fragrant mould.

When heavy on me weighs life's load of care,
Till other touch were more than I could bear,
And o'er my soul there steals a solemn rest,
So sweet it could be none but heavenly guest,
Then know I that the Cross of Calvary's tree
Has cast its healing shade of peace on me.

LENT'S USES.

By Mrs. J. D. H. Browne.

"LIFE has so little joy!" I hear you say,
    "And not a passing hour but brings its trial;
'T is well for those who tread the flowery way,
    To pause awhile and practice self-denial:

"But as for me, it almost makes me smile,
    For all the year is Lent in fullest measure;
Where every day brings with it care and toil,
    Think you the need is great to turn from pleasure?

"Ah! it sounds well, this giving up the world,
    For those whose hearts are sated with its sweetness;
To rest at anchor with the white sails furled,
    Then on again, in sunshine and in fleetness.

"But as for me — I have no time to rest
    And lose myself in saintly contemplation;
No need to fast from what I never taste,
    Or put aside what never *is* temptation."

Ah, friend! it is because your lot is hard,
    Because you walk in dry and stony places,
Because God's precious gift of life is marred,
    And lacks for you its common good and graces,

That I would have you pause, and turn aside
    Into the Lenten shadow, calm and holy,
There for a little blessèd space abide,
    Laying your burden down and kneeling lowly.

For cares, no less than pleasures, may be bars
    To shut out God; and 'neath our burdens bending
We grope our weary way beneath the stars,
    Nor ever see the heavenly light they're lending.

Ah, friend! it is because of way-worn feet
And hearts that hunger for a richer dower
Than toil and care, that there is this retreat,
Where we may learn God's nearness and his power.

Shade of a "Great Rock in a weary land,"
Shade of the Cross, its precious burden bearing!
Here may we learn to grasp the pierced Hand,
And rest upon the Heart our sorrow sharing.

Here learn the awful secret of His Love,
The pity, passing knowledge, still forgiving!
Here find the Peace, which *this* world cannot move,
The joy of loving and the grace of living.

"CLEANSE US, O LORD."

BY ALICE CRARY.

JESUS! our feet are travel-stained and weary
With wand'ring through the self-made path of sin;
Master, the way we trod was long and dreary,
And now we come to Thee, Oh, take us in!

Oh, wash our feet, dear Lord, and turn them homeward;
Thy feet for us toiled up Mount Calvary,
Thy feet for us were pierced in bitter anguish,
Oh, let the precious blood-drops fall on me.

O Christ, these weary hands were used against Thee,
And now, bound fast by Satan, helpless lie;
Begrimed by sin, all torn and bruised and bleeding,
In pity loose and heal them! Hear our cry!

Thy hands, O loving Saviour, toiled for us,
Thy hands, O Jesus, raised the sick and dead.
Thy hands in weakness bore the heavy burden,
Thy hands, O Lord, for us were pierced and bled.

O Christ, behold our heads now bow'd in sorrow:
　　We bring them tired and aching to Thy breast,
The mind obscured by doubts and thoughts of evil;
　　Forgive, O Lord! and give the weary rest.

Thy head, O Jesu, now in glory crownéd,
　　Gave forth the bloody sweat of agony;
And then, dear Lord, with thorny crown encircled,
　　Bowed low, and dying gavest Thy Life for me.

Remember in Thy kingdom, Lord, Thy passion,
　　Remember, too, our human frailty,
And in Thy mercy, grant Thy absolution
　　And give Thy strength that we may conquerors be.

Oh, wash us, Lord, and cleanse us from all evil,
　　From strength to strength lead us, dear Lord, we pray.
That in this world our part of loving service
　　May win the Part that fadeth not away.

———

HUMILITY.

By Marion Couthouy Smith.

OH, last, best grace of all!
　　When we have striv'n to soar in pride and strength
　　Toward glorious heights of soul, serenely fair,
　　Dreaming to dwell thus in a pure air,
But our poor wings have failed — how sweet at length
　　To let the struggle go, and in Thine Arms to fall!

　　But teach me, Lord, while yet I can withstand —
Ere I must drop, for very weariness,
　　And failure's cruel stress —
　　Now to fly low, and lay my strength and pride
Down in the hollow of Thy pierced Hand,
　　For love alone, since Thou my King wert crucified.

THE STATIONS OF THE CROSS.

BY WILLIAM B. CHISHOLM.

THY Lord's last weary hours,
    Before thee on the canvas luminous,
Speak to thy heart amid these gaudy bowers,
Amid the maze of earthly leaves and flowers.
    The sight of Him, the Lamb Vicarious,
    Who is the Very Paschal Lamb for us,
May sober thee; and lift thy earth-bent eye
To gaze upon this last great mystery.

Behold the awful passage up the hill!
Dost thou discern one ray of sympathy?
Look at that Roman sentinel! He stands
Poising his spear between his horny hands,
Spear that shall pierce the Mediator's side,
Spear that to crown transformed is glorified
In this thy gaze; it pierced thy Lord, but then
That Blood redeemed thee. Even so, Amen.

Oh, Simon of Cyrene! seems it hard
    That thou awhile must bear that heavy load,
While He of Nazareth shall seize brief rest?
    Prouder than laurel wreath that decks the bard,
Or star-gemmed crown upon dead hero's breast,
    Be this to thee! Go hence to thine abode
Tear-dimmed; yet like a conquering monarch go,
With this one thought: that thou hast borne for Him
For one brief spell the burden that shall lift
    All other weight from lost humanity.
Whereon shall hang the harps of seraphim
    In the immortal ages yet to be;
There, there it stands at noon-day strange and dim,
    An awful portent 'gainst the darkened sky,
    Yet is it life and light and victory!

O thou, august o'er all sweet womanhood,
Thou ever blest and ever holy one,
Gazing, tear-dimmed, upon thy bleeding Son,
Behold thy King! and in this beam of wood
On which a bleeding Sufferer He hangs,
Forget, O Virgin blest! a mother's pangs,
And mortal yet, and human e'en as we,
Low at His Cross behold the Deity!

O sun of Judah, veil thy stricken face!
  O graves, give forth your olden, saintly dead;
O temple veil, in sunder rent, give place
  To His new temple of the heart and life!
  Past is the awful strife;
  The sacrifice complete;
At morning, where the angel hosts have led
  To His dear tomb, prepare your King to greet!

THE ANNUNCIATION OF THE BLESSED VIRGIN MARY.

By M. A. T.

THROUGH the sins and sorrows
　Of four thousand years,
Earth has watched and waited,
　Smiling through her tears;
Watched to greet the dawning
　Of a brighter morn;
Waited for a Saviour,
　Man, of woman born.

Now the blessed Dayspring
　Cometh from on high;
Now the world's Redeemer.
　To her aid draws nigh;
Bearer of the tidings,
　From the throne of light,
To a lowly maiden,
　Speeds an angel bright.

In the chosen daughter
　Of King David's line,
God fulfils the promise
　Of King Ahaz' sign.
Gabriel hath spoken;
　Mary hath believed;
And, behold, a virgin
　Hath a Son conceived!

Earthly sire He hath not;
　For the promised rod
Of the stem of Jesse
　Is the Son of God;

Virgin pure the temple
  Where He lies enshrined,
Holy One of Jacob,
  Hope of all mankind !

Though He take our nature,
  Linked to low estate,
Though He stoop to suffer,
  Yet shall He be great;
Though His crown and sceptre
  Be of thorn and reed;
His shall be the kingdom,
  Sworn to David's seed.

Light to lighten the Gentiles
  Bending at His throne:
Glory of His people,
  When His sway they own.
He shall reign forever,
  King of kings confessed;
And all tribes and kindreds
  Shall, in Him, be blest.

Through the brightened ages,
  O'er the ransomed earth,
All shall bless and honor
  Her who gave Him birth;
Her of whom, incarnate,
  Came the Lord of all,
To uplift creation
  From the primal fall.

THE ANNUNCIATION.

By William B. Chisholm.

HAIL! beauteous Mother! Hail!
    Wealth and bloom we bring to thee,
Ere yet the wondrous tale
    Rings over earth and sea,
Blest be thou, o'er all earth's daughters blest!
Gladly now our hearts proclaim Annunciation's feast.

Upon thy virgin brow
    Sits innocence enthroned;
And motherhood's sweet presence now
    Its lighter lines have toned;
Thou hast no jasper palace trod nor unveiled glories seen;
Yet o'er thee rests the aureole of heaven's unstinted sheen.

Hail! fair Madonna! Hail!
    O'er all thy sisterhood,
Transcendent image of the true,
    The beautiful, the good;
All generations shall rise up and welcome thee the blest,
As in the holy calendar that heralds thy high feast.

THE LORD IS RISEN.

By J. J. L. England.

OUR hearts with bitter grief were sad
            But yesterday;
This morn rejoicing they are glad,
For Christ hath risen from the dead,
And Death and Hell are captive led!

The sealéd stone before the tomb
            Is rolled away!
Light piercing through its deepest gloom
Reveals no captive in that prison,
For lo! the Lord of Life hath risen!

Where now thy victory, O Grave?
            Or, Death, thy sting?
Jesus with mighty power to save,
He Who on yonder cross was slain,
Hath risen from the dead again!

Shout, all ye glad angelic throng,
            And mortals too!
Join ye in one triumphant song,
The Lord hath risen from the dead!
The Lord hath risen as He said!

Wide let the glorious anthem roll,
  In loud acclaim !
Circling the earth from pole to pole,
Till far and wide the tidings spread,
The Lord hath risen from the dead !

EASTER MORN.

By Amelia Truesdell.

CHRIST'S woe is done ! Let Easter sun
  Shout "glorias" to the morn!
For now on earth in second birth
 The Promised One is born.

The smitten grave its Prisoner gave,
 Nor dares to claim Him — dead ;
For glory shone on virgin stone
 Where lay th' anointed Head.

The purple scorn, the plaited thorn,
 For Him beloved are o'er ;
The hour of gloom, the cry of doom,
 Shall bow the heavens no more.

From seraph throngs grand Easter songs
 Ring out through all the spheres ;
For now is done the work begun
 In Judah's vale of tears.

Then bind the cross with softest moss,
 And wreathe with garlands round :
Put lilies fair in chaplets where
 That radiant head was bound.

Aye, sing on earth this heavenly birth,
    That all shall live who died,
That Christ has risen, that Death's dark prison
    His form has glorified.

And answer loud, ye faithful "cloud
    Of witnesses " above;
Low at his feet the song repeat
    Of Jesus' Easter love.

———————

EASTER THOUGHTS.

By the Rev. W. E. Snowden.

IN the spring morn the Easter bells
    From town and hamlet tower,
Cathedral domes and lowly dells,
    Their joyous anthems pour.
Ring out, ye bells, your cantinells!
    Air, with the music quiver!
Christ in the tomb no longer dwells;
    He lives and reigns forever.

All the wide air is full of sound,
    Rejoicing, triumphing;
The hills give back the glad rebound,
    The Easter carolling.
The teeming earth looks up to-day
    To greet her risen Lord;
The buds swell and the year's decay
    Lives at His quickening word.

As erst in Bethany He stood
    Beside the silent tomb,
His voice gave life its plenitude
    Within that darkened room,

So ever in His universe,
In all the bounds of time,
All things His living power rehearse
And feel His life sublime.

Because He lives they also live,
Because He rose they rise.
Each spring each flower their virtues give,
And Easter prophecies.
The ice, the winter's frozen breath,
A living flood shall be,
Springing exulting from its death
And sparkling to the sea.

The sleep that lies, a lethal veil,
On man from eve till morn
Is broken by the sun's " All hail! "
We rise, to life reborn.
The showy plant in all its pride
Fell with the year's decay.
Root hid in earth and seed that died
Now feel the Easter ray;

And lo! a fairer, other growth,
Other and yet the same,
Risen from earth in glorious youth,
Shall Easter truth proclaim.
The chrysalis in loathly shell
Its poor dull life lays down;
We seek its dead within that cell, —
" 'T is not there; " it has flown!

A butterfly, with plumage bright,
It swims in upper air
From the dark prison of its night,
And keeps its Easter there.
The chrysalis to death is given,
The shell bursts, and a thing
Of beauty scales the airs of heaven
With never-tiring wing.

THE BLESSED MORN.

By R. L. Argent.

FROM sin's dark, gloomy prison-house we rise
 Into the freedom of a purer air, —
A freedom none of earthly mould may share
Save who have offered willing sacrifice
  Of self and sense.

From dreams of doubt and darkness we awake
 To see the lamps of hope and joy alight, —
 To view the world in rarer raiment dight
And feel, as we of heaven's grace partake,
  New life from thence.

The Easter sunlight floods earth's utmost length,
 The Easter blooms make all ways fragrant-fair,
 The Easter bells proclaim upon the air, —
" All Easter blessings flow from Him, our strength
  And our defence !"

EASTER SONG.

By Annie Ellicott.

BIRD in the zenith, airily circling,
 Why upward thy flight and so joyful thy lay ?
Cometh the answer, thrilling with rapture,
 " The Saviour hath risen !   'T is Easter to-day !"

Flowers, the woodland gemming so brightly,
 Why waken ye now ?   'T will be long 'ere 't is May.
Wind-bent, the blossoms joyfully murmur,
 " The Saviour hath risen !   'T is Easter to-day !"

Breezes, why blow ye, so softly, so gently?
Why linger not here with the grasses to play?
" Hymns from the earth to heaven we are wafting!
The Saviour hath risen! 'T is Easter to-day!"

Soul, when the birds, and the flowers, and the breezes
Praises are singing, earth-bound will you stay?
Join in the anthem that rises to heaven,
" The Saviour hath risen! 'T is Easter to-day!"

AN EASTER SONG.

By Callie L. Bonney.

IN shade of death the world doth sleep,
While white-robed angels vigils keep
    O'er stone-bound tomb;
And night-winds whisper requiem low,
While shadowy forms flit to and fro
    'Mid cypress gloom.

When lo! a heavenly radiance falls,
Reflected from the jasper walls,
    Where pearl-gate gleams :
The heavy stone is rolled away,
While dawning resurrection day
    With glory teems.

No more the cypress and the tomb,
Where now immortal flowers bloom,
    Bright, fair, alway;
Life's King, in majesty divine,
Makes resurrection blessing thine,
    On Easter Day.

"IT IS THE LORD'S PASSOVER."

BY THE REV. ELI CHRYSOSTOM BURR.

ALL hail, dear Risen Lord! all hail!
   'T is past, the grave, the cross, the nail;
'T is past. the breaking hearts, the wail;
      Alleluia!

All hail, dear Risen Lord! no trace
Of Calvary's woe hath marred Thy face.
All hail! Redeemer of our race!
      Alleluia!

We sought Thy grave, and angels cried:
" Ye seek Him who was crucified;
Behold! He is risen, glorified."
      Alleluia!

On Friday, — darkness. death, the tomb!
To-day, — light, life, and Paschal bloom!
The Risen Christ hath chased the gloom.
      Alleluia!

The new-born earth, in spring array,
With full, adoring love doth pray
Beneath Thy nail-pierced feet to-day.
    Alleluia !

"What mean ye by this service?" cries
The wondering world ; the Church replies :
"It is the Lord Christ's Sacrifice."
    Alleluia !

Angels who throng the starry ways
Take up the glorious strain we raise,
And Heaven's foundations shake with praise.
    Alleluia !

EASTER.

By Edward Hyacinth Tottenham.

NOW does old hoary winter, faltering,
    Retrace his footprints to the icy North ;
And many a guerdon of long-wished-for Spring
    O'er hill and dale is gently budding forth.

But yesterday the solemn Lenten fast
    Did bow the head and make the bright eye dim ;
So has the Lenten *Miserere* passed
    To the fair lustre of the Easter hymn.

We live two lives upon this little earth, —
    One life around us, and one life above :
Flowers, and birds, and our immortal souls,
    Are all controlléd by one hand of love.

Chase then thy cares ; and with untiring wing,
    Fly with thy sins to Jesus' wounded side :
So shall thy life be one perpetual Spring,
    Thy death, an everlasting Easter-tide.

AN EASTER HYMN.

By the Rev. H. G. Batterson, D. D.

ALLELUIA! Alleluia!
    Alleluia sing to-day!
Christ has opened death's dark prison,
    Bright the tomb wherein He lay.
Sing with gladness, Alleluia!
    He has brought Eternal day.

Sing, ye Christians, Alleluia!
    Darkness from the grave hath fled;
Sing ye joyous Alleluia!
    Christ is now our King and Head;
Lift your song with thankful voices,
    He is risen from the dead!

Sing, all nations, Alleluia!
    Christ is victor o'er the grave;
Sing again loud Alleluia!
    He has passed through Jordan's wave;
Oh, how glorious is the triumph!
    He is mighty now to save!

Sing once more the Alleluia!
    In this happy Easter-tide;
Sing, undaunted, Alleluia!
    Now is healed the Wounded Side;
Christ, of death the First-Begotten,
    Is our Brother, Friend, and Guide.

Bring the lilies, bring the roses,
    Let the altar gleam with light;
Shout with rapture, Alleluia!
    Christ has conquered death and night;
He, our Paschal Lamb, will feed us,
    Guard us, keep us, in His might!

BRIGHT EASTER SKIES.

BY THE RT. REV. ALEX. BURGESS, D.D.

BRIGHT Easter skies !
　　Fair Easter skies !
Our Lord is risen ;
We too shall rise.
Nor walls of stone hewn firm and cold,
Nor Roman soldiers brave and bold,
Nor Satan's marshalled hosts could keep
The piercéd hands in deathly sleep ;
Just as the Easter day-beams dawn
Our buried Lord is risen and gone !

　　Loud Easter bells !
　　Rich Easter bells !
　　A ransomed world
　　Your chiming tells.
Let hills and rocks your gladness peal !
Behold the stone and broken seal !
Angels in white from heaven's bright way
The useless clothes together lay,
Then sit serene at head and feet
The earliest saints with joy to greet.

　　Green Easter fields !
　　Fair Easter fields !
　　Heaven's first ripe fruit
　　Death conquered yields.
In churchyards wide the seeds we sow ;
Beneath the Cross the wheat shall grow :
One Easter Day Death's reign shall end,
And golden sheaves shall heavenward send.
Hail the blest morn, by whose glad light
Angels shall reap the harvest white !

Sweet Easter flowers !
White Easter flowers !
From heaven descend
Life-giving showers.
Each plant that bloomed at Eden's birth
Shall blow again o'er ransomed earth.
Pluck lilies rare and roses sweet,
And strew the path of Jesus' feet ;
Throw fragrant palms before our King,
And wreathe the crown the saved shall bring !

O Christian child !
O Christian men !
Our Victor Lord
Shall come again.
Wake we our hearts at His command ;
Lift we our love to His right hand ;
With warmest hopes, to Easter skies,
Stretch we our arms and fix our eyes ;
Till in the clouds His sign we see,
And quick and dead shout jubilee !

THE GENTLE STRANGER.

By the Rev. R. W. Lowrie, D.D.

ALONG Judea's twilight way
      The two communed with bated breath.
Three days had lapsed, with rayless skies,
      Since Jesus' death.

The while to sober language given,
      A gentle Stranger draws Him near;
But eye was blind; His usual voice,
      Nor heard the ear.

In accents mild and musical,
   The Stranger, as they walked apace:
" What converse this that hold ye twain ?
   Why sad of face ? "

Then answered Cleopas, and said:
   " A Stranger art Thou in the land,
And knowest not the grievous things
   At present hand ? "

Then all the Scriptures, as they went,
   Of Moses, and of prophets old,
In full recital, wondrous plain,
   The Stranger told.

And now have Emmaus' lamps, like stars,
   Shone softly thro' the even-tide ;
The Stranger hastens ; but they said :
   " With us abide."

Delaying at their sweet request,
   The Stranger sat Him down at meat ;
And bread He took, and blessed and brake.
   And gave to eat.

Their eyes no longer holden were,
   For fell the scales from off the sight ;
But scarce they knew the Lord, until
   He vanished quite !

" Did not our hearts within us burn,
   As never burned our hearts before,
The while He opened, by the way,
   The Sacred Lore ? "

And, lo, with steps retraced, they tell
   The wondrous things the Stranger said ;
And how the Risen Lord was known.
   In breaking bread !

THE CONVERSION OF THE CENTURION.

(The Day after the Resurrection.)

BY THE RT. REV. W. E. McLAREN, D.D., D.C.L.

THOU say'st He is arisen? that Nazarene
　　Whom they did roughly crown with thorns, whose
　　　　side
I pierced with this good spear of mine, alive?
By Mars, I marvel at thy word.　Go to,
Thou trembling subject of a vanquished king!
Nor mock me with thy story of a death
That was not death, a tomb that was no tomb;
Thy grief to folly hath transformed thy wit
And made thee babble.　Mock me not, O Jew!

And yet do I remember all that scene,
The evening of your Sabbath, when He died.
A shudder ran through nature, rocks were rent,
And it is whispered that your temple's veil
Was cleft in twain, and the black heavens frowned,
As if one of the immortal gods had died.

I am a man of blood, these eyes have gazed
On many a crucifixion of the unjust;
These ears have heard their cries of agony;
And, truth to say, this heart familiar grown
With death, has lost the natural tenderness
Of man.　But ne'er saw I a death like His,
Which made that heart a woman's, soft with flow
Of sympathetic grief.　Give me thine ear,
For I am burdened with emotions strange,
Nor can their hidden meaning comprehend.

My men had raised Him on the painful wood,
And, as we use, had gambled for His robe;
When, with a pitiful voice He cried aloud
To One whom we saw not.　" Father," He said,

" Forgive them, for they know not what they do ! "
It struck me to the depths.   I could not deem
This man was worthy of the cruel strokes
Of Roman hammers on our sharpen'd nails,
Nor of the deadlier thrust of priestly scorn
And bitter piercing of Sanhedrim hate.
What manner of man is this — such was my thought —
Who answers ribald mockings with a prayer,
And mingles pardons with His dropping blood ?

Three hours He hung upon the cross — three hours
Of sharper agony than tongue can tell,
Three hours, O Jew, made beautiful with love.
He pardoned us, He comforted a thief,
He blessed three women standing close with one
Whose moan revealed a mother's bleeding heart,
Pierced with a keener sword than this I wear.
One day, at Vesta's shrine in Rome, I saw —
Her veil withdrawn — a virgin-priestess' face,
Too fair, I thought, for eyes like mine to see ;
I tell thee, Jew, more beautiful than she
Was that sad woman wailing at the cross.
May Vesta soothe her !

                    At the hour of noon
Thick darkness crept upon Jerusalem
And rested thickest on Golgotha's height.
Loud-voiced the sufferer on Elias called,
Who came not.   With our soldier's wine we sought,
Lifting a hyssop-stem, to quench his thirst,
And all the earth seem'd trembling with despair.
Then Jesus bowed His head and died.   O'erwhelmed
I cried : In truth He was a son of God !

What frenzy hath o'ercome thy nation, Jew,
That they invoke such blood upon their heads —
The blood of one so innocent, so good ?
Oh, had our Pilate known this godlike man
As I do seem to know, he ne'er had bid
My band to do this awful deed.

7

Alive?

Thou say'st He is alive? His sepulchre
Untenanted? What means this whisper'd tale
Of magic sages never dreamed could be?
They tell us death is not the end of life,
And I, though rude in speech, unskilled in thought,
Have in my simpler way attained the height
Of their philosophy; for how can man
Deny the immortal longings of his soul,
Or deem the arch of life to rest alone
Upon the column that we see. Beyond --
'T is thus I argue — stands the other shaft
Built on the Eternal Rock. But who dare dream
That they who pass can evermore return?

If e'er by favor of the immortal gods
One perished body were to burst its tomb,
I could imagine this strong Son of God,
This king of thine, might win the awful boon, —
He was so noble! on His brow was set
The signet of a soul so unearthly pure!
If my unwilling spear, obedient
To stern command of law, pierc'd my own side
With sharper pang than his, if in the gloom
Of the sixth hour I curs'd my fate that I,
A sinful man, could not this hero save,
I think the Pitiful Ones who dwell above
Would bend to listen to His dying cry
And by some portent justify His prayer.
Yea, if, indignant grown, the onlooking powers
Should give him back what Hebrew malice took,
And if the " Father " God, on whom He called,
Should bid corruption's worm to touch Him not,
I could believe it — will believe it true.

Perchance, — is 't not a thought, O Jew, to thrill
Our souls? — perchance this man was more than man,
A god come down to show some better way
For men to live that live, for men that die
To die, — a god more strong than life, than death,

Than the all-conquering grave.   Perchance
This messenger of better things shall speak
When Pan is dead and Jupiter himself
Shall lose his grasp on thunderbolts of wrath ;
'T is said our oracles grow dumb ; and I
Have heard prophetic whispers, speeding far
O'er all the empire, that a new age comes —
Another chapter in Time's fateful book.
It may be true.   Nay, by my heart's strange leap,
I cannot choose but hail the better day,
Brought nigh by Him who died and rose again.

Lead me, O Jew, where I may worship Him —
Brother of mine, oh, lead me to the spot
Where we may learn more of that Father-love,
Of holy pardon and the immortal life,
Of death that is not death, of graves where we
Shall only sleep a little while !

                         No more
Relentless Mars, spear-armed, dare I invoke —
Before the Conqueror of Death I bow !

THE ASCENSION.

By the Rev. C. W. Leffingwell, D.D.

LIFT up your heads, O gates! Be lifted high,
Ye everlasting portals of the sky!
The King, in glorious majesty draws nigh!

He comes with power, who lived on earth unknown,
Despised by men, rejected by His own;
He comes, a King, victorious to His throne.

The Lord ascends! His work on earth is done;
The Lord ascends! His reign in Heaven begun, —
His people ransomed and His kingdom won.

Sing, O ye heavens! Be joyful all ye lands!
O all ye people, shout, and clap your hands!
High over all the King of Glory stands!

Who is the King of glory? Even He,
The Lord of Hosts, who evermore shall be! —
The risen Lord, who ruleth land and sea!

O earth, rejoice! Ye isles thereof, be glad!
O suffering world, so long oppressed and sad,
Behold your King, in strength and beauty clad!

Behold your King, though passed from human sight, —
By faith behold Him, — where in regal might,
He comes, a conqueror, to His throne of light!

Lift up your heads, O gates! Wide open swing,
Ye doors of Heaven! While men and angels sing
A loud hosanna to the glorious King!

THE ASCENSION.

By W. B. Chisholm.

TO rise, O Lord, with Thee, —
To leave low earth, its sorrows and its joys,
Wearied with toilsome sport, with fleeting toys,
Fain to ascend where angel's harp employs
Its sweetest note to sing Thy glorious praise,
Behold, O Lord, worn with these dusty ways,
I would ascend with Thee!

But I must grovel here, yet see Thee go;
Yearn, with fast-dimming gaze, as up the track
Of yonder sky Thy bright ascension shows
To my sad feet their feebleness, — no wings,
Naught, naught but grief and vexedness, below, —
Yet hear the gentle mandate hastening back,
All fraught with soul-reviving cheer,
            "Press on!
The path of pain and toil is still the way;
Bide on the heavenly promise, — breaks the day."

But, Lord, I weary grow!
I see bright-vested angels girt to wait
Around Thy kingly feast, still hard and late
I toil for grace.   Yet passion charms to sin;
And sin to death will drag. Can I not go?
Is this Thy will, — this lonely walk below?

"Yes, restless heart, believe thou, — BUT BELIEVE!
When I am ready thou shalt hear thy call.
Keep faithful fast!   Anon the festival
Shall peal its bells for thee.   Nor grieve
That e'en the friend thou lov'st most dear must go
Before thy soul's release; abide below
All dutiful and murmurless.   Ere long
My voice shall bid thee join the holy throng!"

WHITSUNTIDE LILIES.

By N. M. Hitchcock.

R ING out your dainty bells, ye lilies of the valley
  With tender grace!
With loveliness most fit adorn the font, the altar,
  The holy place!

Ring out your tender bells, ye quivering, wind-blown lilies,
  While we rejoice
In Him who comes alike in rushing wind and mighty,
  And still small voice!

Ring out your bells so pure, ye fair, ye snowy lilies!
  The Holy Dove,
To make our hearts as white and to present us spotless,
  Comes from above.

Ring out your chalice-bells, ye incense-wafting lilies!
  Your perfumed breath
Shall tell of offering pure from hearts the Spirit's pleading
  Has waked from death.

Ring out your blessed bells, ye Pentecostal lilies!
  The Paraclete,
The Comforter is come!   Oh, be our hearts his dwelling,
  His temple meet.

THANKSGIVING HYMN.

By the Rev. John Anketell.

GOD of our fathers, enthroned through all ages,
    Ever in mercy and kindness revealed,
Guard us in peace : and when war's tumult rages
    Be Thou our helmet, our sword, and our shield.

Through the long years Thou hast granted us blessing,
    Filling our homes with the light of Thy grace :
Let us as children, Thy love still possessing,
    Ever rejoice in the smile of Thy face.

When the fierce tempest around us is raving,
    Let the wild storm be restrained by Thy will, —
As on the lake, where the white crests were waving
    O'er the rough billows, Thy voice cried, " Be still!"

Crown our broad prairies with sheaves rich and golden,
    Fill all our dwellings with plenty and health;
Let our fair children. as in the days olden,
    Find in Thy blessing their joy and their wealth.

Still with Thy wisdom our senators guiding,
    Grant to our warriors a heart brave and true :
O'er the wide ocean let proud navies riding
    Show to the nations our Red, White, and Blue.

Guard well our Union unmoved and unshaken;
    Love be the bond that shall bind us as one.
Safe is our trust, by Thine arm unforsaken;
    Shine on us ever, Eternity's Sun.

God of our fathers, enthroned through all ages,
    Low at Thy footstool our homage we yield :
Guard us in peace ; and when fierce battle rages
    Be Thou our helmet, our sword, and our shield.

ALL SAINTS' DAY.

By Katherine A. Matthew.

OUR year wanes fast; and the rain-drops fall,
   As though Nature were tired and grieving;
The pale sun shines through a golden mist
   On the scenes it will soon be leaving.

Our hearts beat slowly, life's pulses chill,
   Looking back on the year departed, —
The year that we met in its Easter joy,
   Faithful and happy-hearted.

Now slowly and solemnly over our heads
   The All-Saints' bells are swinging;
And our hands are folded for purer prayer
   While the heavenward chime is ringing.

Into her wide, kind, loving arms,
   The Church our Mother, enfolding,
Comforting, bids us lift our eyes,
   New life, new joys, beholding.

Her year wanes too; and her message sweet
   Lies soft on our hearts' complaining,
Like the gentle grace of the summer glow
   On the fair, clear sky remaining.

" Let the dead past be dead ! " she breathes,
   " Child of my love unfailing.
Look on to the light of the Advent morn !
   Faith is not unavailing."

" Ah ! but our souls are stained with sin
   For which there is no forgiving, —
Promises broken, neglected vows,
   And life's unworthiest living."

" For ye, tired children, sorrowful ones,
    The message is ever given, —
Pardon and Love again and again
    Till your sins' last chain is riven.

" Pray — for the Master will come full soon ;
    Watch — for his reappearing ;
Trust — for His word is ever true ;
    Hope — for the skies are clearing.

" Into the glorious Advent light,
    Solemn and steadfast shining,
Lift up your hearts, — be strong, be true,
    Work, love, trust, unrepining ;

" For the saints, whose glorious lives ye read,
    Sinned too, and were God-forgiven, —
Finished their work and kept the faith ;
    And for them the rest of Heaven."

ALL SAINTS' DAY.

BY THE REV. M. LINDSAY KELLNER.

FOR all Thy Saints in Paradise, the bless'd,
    Whose footsteps once these pilgrim pathways pressed,
Who have attained to Thy dear land of rest,
    Alleluia ! Lord, to Thee.

For Thine Apostles, guileless, eager, bold,
Who truly shepherded their Master's fold ;
For Martyrs dying for the crown foretold,
    Alleluia ! Lord, to Thee.

For Thine Evangelists, with heavenly might,
By Holy Ghost inspired the Word to write,
Mid earth's dark skies the one, the hallowed Light,
    Alleluia ! Lord, to Thee.

For God-sent Priests, who taught their fellow-men
To love Thy precepts, from their sins refrain,
And turned their wayward steps to Thee again,
  Alleluia! Lord, to Thee.

For saintly Fathers, who have crossed the flood,
And left these weary ways which once they trod,
Whose souls undying now are with their God,
  Alleluia! Lord, to Thee.

For gentle Mothers, home divinely led,
Whose angel-faces smiling bend to shed
A benediction on their children's head,
  Alleluia! Lord, to Thee.

For these, a glorious band forever bless'd,
The Church triumphant, Church with Thee at rest,
Forever through the ages be addressed
  Alleluia! Lord, to Thee.

WITHIN THE VEIL.

By N. M. HITCHCOCK.

WHEN the autumn's glowing splendor
    Softens in the haze so tender
      Of the Indian-summer skies,
Then my soul, her eyes upraising,
Through the veil would fain be gazing
      On the hills of Paradise.

For the Church now tells the story
Of the blessed ones in glory,
      Tasting joys that never fail;
Of the multitude unnumbered,
Who, no more by cares encumbered,
      Dwell with Christ within the veil.

Purple tints are softly gleaming
On the hills ; and, to my seeming,
    At this holy All-Saints' tide,
Through the mists come faintly swelling
Strains of sweetest music, telling
How the saints in glory dwelling
    Join to praise the Crucified.

Earth grows dim and Heaven seems nearer ;
To faith's vision grows yet clearer
    The bright fields of Paradise,
Where is blessedness supernal,
Where are pastures ever vernal,
Where the flowers bloom eternal,
    And the streams immortal rise.

Nor shall fade the vision glorious,
Till o'er sin and hell victorious,
    Christ shall all things good perfect ;
Ours the hope of blessed union,
Ours the mystical communion,
    With the hosts of God's elect.

Thus may we, in faith abiding,
Follow the Good Shepherd's guiding,
    Falter not, though hosts assail ;
Till, the palms of victory bearing,
Amaranthine garlands wearing,
Our Redeemer's victory sharing,
    We shall dwell within the veil.

AGNUS DEI.

By Isabel G. Eaton.

O LAMB of God!
With sins bowed down, I cry!
The woes that mortals bear till day of doom,
The web of grief woven in life's weird loom,
Like shadows swiftly fly
When Jesus passeth by.

O Lamb of God!
Before Thine altar fair
The prayers of saints, like incense, ever soar.
The Eternal Son, in love forevermore
Veils His bright glory there.
And bends our griefs to share.

O Lamb of God!
For us the Feast is spread.
Not all in vain Thy bitter cross and woe
When from it wells of living water flow ;
The wine glows ruby red,
And thus Thy blood was shed.

O Lamb of God!
Who tak'st our sins away!
Thy mercy show to souls all penitent
Who seek Thee in this Blessed Sacrament.
Thou Sun of perfect day!
Shine on our toilsome way!

O Lamb of God!
The soul no pain may bear
Who finds Thee in the Church's sacred feast,
For at Thy Word the waves' wild tumult ceased,
    And peace fell like a prayer.
    Shall we Thy sorrows share,
    O Lamb of God?

HOLY COMMUNION HYMN.

By JOHN C. GARRETT.

DEAR Jesus, full of tender grace.
    In homage low we kneel.
To glimpse the brightness of Thy face.
    Which outward signs reveal.

Faith proves Thee present, Lord Divine:
    By faith then to us come:
Conveyed by creatures — bread and wine —
    Make in our hearts Thy home.

The broken Body we receive.
    We drink Thy Life's pure flow:
Now cleanse us from the guilt we grieve,
    In peace then bid us go.

Shadows, we know, must now divide,
    Between our sight and Thee;
Yet, through them, we approach Thy side,
    And prove Thy grace so free.

Dear Saviour, Jesus, Holy Guest,
    To us now deign to come;
In our poor hearts shed peace, give rest —
    Sweet antepast of Home.

Yea, Lord, " in this sweet morning hour "
　Thyself to us impart;
Thee to receive, bestow the power,
　And fill our empty heart.

EARLY COMMUNION.

By O. W. Rogers.

A T day's sweet prime I seek the fane,
　　Lord, where Thine honor dwells.
The sunshine through the painted pane
　A glorious day foretells ;
And lights upon the altar shine
As heralds of Thy grace divine.

Peace welcomes me.   I leave behind
　The world and worldly ways;
With childlike and receptive mind
　I come to pray and praise. —
To see Thee "lifted up," O Lord,
By faithful souls to be adored.

I lay upon Thine altar fair,
　As offering, my heart;
My sins I plead : they many are :
　Their pardon, Lord, impart,
And so refresh me with Thy grace
That I may better run life's race.

For those in Paradise I plead,
　Who in the flesh were dear ;
For loved ones absent intercede,
　As they were kneeling here.
O sweetest Feast !   Communion blest,
　'T is *here* we meet and in Thee rest.

O make us all partakers, Lord,
  Of Thy dear Self to be ;
Our hearts engraven with Thy Word,
  Our lives Thy ministry,
And ever thankful for Thy love,
So freely given us to prove.

The priest bestows the sign of grace,
  The Benedicite,
While silence fills the holy place
  Where God is wont to be,
And then my pilgrim path I take
Ere yet the world is quite awake.

OUR LORD IN THE BLESSED SACRAMENT.

By Marion Couthouy Smith.

HE came in the morning, sweet and still
  As the first sun-ray on some lonely hill ;
From the splendor of heaven, from the awful throne,
Veiled and silent, He came alone.

And the few glad hearts that looked for Him,
In the pure, soft hush of the morning dim,
Had raised Him an altar, and made it bright
With the loveliest gifts, — with flowers and light.

But because He came in such lowliness,
How many souls whom He willed to bless
Looked out beyond Him, and would not own
Their very King on so poor a throne !

The angels owned Him, an unseen throng ;
But the silence stirred not with cry or song :
The great world slumbered, and none drew near
But the few to whom He was more than dear, —

The few from whose eyes no veil could hide
The Being of Him once crucified;
And into their heart of hearts He came,
And met and mingled as flame with flame.

But some — oh, wonder ! — could touch Him so
With soul and body, and *never know*,
Nor think, nor care how His wondrous Love
Drew Him with yearning from heights above.

Daily it draws Him, — so still, so sweet!
Though few should own Him, though none should greet.
With us forever He wills to stay;
Jesu, Rex gloriæ, adoro Te !

THE HOLY EUCHARIST.

By the Rev. F. S. Jewell, Ph.D.

THE holy ground on which we reverent tread
    With shrinking foot-fall and unsandalled feet;
The mystic shrine within whose vale we meet
The wondrous presence of our gracious Head :
The altar at whose blood-stained base we bend
    With grateful alms and holy praise and prayer ;
    The Table in whose feast we thankful share;
The riches which the Master's grace attend, —
    All these, with light and life and love, are thine :
    O Sacrament of Sacrifice divine !

EUCHARISTIC HYMN.

By Wm. E. Snowden.

PANIS mundi date mundo
Immundis hominibus,
Nos coelesti Cibo Tuo,
Pastor, Panis, pasce nos,

Vinum animæ perdignum,
Agne Dei, Domine,
Ferens plagas supra Lignum,
Ligno latus, nos audi.

Panis fracte supra Lignum,
Panis Tu ex Arbore,
Opem fer iis qui dignum
Coena veniunt frui.

Sanguis fuse supra Lignum,
Agne pro nobis Dei,
Castos fac eos qui dignum
Coena veniunt frui.

Sanguis sacer sacræ Vitis,
Quo rei queunt lui,
Veniam da his contritis
Coena qui eunt frui.

Sacra Vitis, Vinum sacrum
Vitam nostro corpori
Animæque ferto Tuam,
Coena quum imus frui.

Panis mundi, Vitis, Vinum,
Pastor, Pastus, nos imple
Te Ipso. Da nobis plenum
Donum Tui, Domine.

THE BREAD OF LIFE.

By Jennie Marsh Parker.

DEAR Lord, and can it be
    That Thou hast bidden me
To break my fast, my hungry soul to fill,
    With that blest company
    In heaven's purity, —
The host of angels, loyal to Thy will?

    I know it is not meet
    That one whose sinful feet
Are ever prone to choose the evil way,
    Should come Thy courts within
    From where these feet have been.
"Come unto me," Thou sayest: I obey.

    And, dear Lord, as I come
    Let all of earth be dumb,
That my vexed soul Thy temple calm may be,
    And yearning to be fed
    Of Thee, the living Bread, —
A sweet foretaste of heaven and of Thee.

    O blessed company,
    Enwrapt in ecstasy,
What place have I where angel's food is given?
    "Lift up your hearts," he saith;
    "Nor hunger unto death, —
One Bread I break for all of earth and heaven."

EUCHARISTIC LIVES.

BY THE REV. J. HEBER MCCANDLESS.

(Gospel for the Fourteenth Sunday after Trinity.)

D ISTRESS unites and moves the ten to pray
And lift their voices to the Lord :
Relief divides, and scatters each his way,
Unmindful of a thankful word ;
While wounded Love, in sad and wondering tone,
In reverie, as though alone,
Beholding only *one* who kneeled,
Speaks to ungrateful hearts, " Were not *ten* healed? "

A stranger to God's Church and lawful Priest
Comes near to Christ, and with loud voice
Gives praise and thanks ; for he at least
In light will gratefully rejoice.
All healed, in Eucharistic song he lays
At Jesus' feet his praise,
Adoring lowly Him who blest
And filled in love his soul with deepest rest.

O loving Christ, what mercies day by day
Poured from Thy hands around us fall !
But where are hearts that in thanksgiving pray?
Dost come to Thee one tenth of all ?
Our souls lift up a moaning voice in prayer, —
" Kyrie Eleison ! Spare ! "
Love hears ; and gracious voices come.
Eucharistic then our lives ? or are they dumb?

O souls, absolved by Christ's most gracious word,
Made pure and clean, and filled with gladness,
When at the font and altar prayer He heard,
Seek Him, and keep His heart from sadness !
Seek Eucharist, and keep His love,
And live with Him above !
And at the altar, with most thankful heart,
Draw near, where nine from ten depart.

Consolation.

Poems of Consolation.

"THERE WAS NO MORE SEA."

By Thomas Mair.

Bright on the dark, retreating clouds,
  Through drops that sparkle in the sunlight's glow,
Spanning the east, we view displayed
  In calm, pure beauty, God's majestic bow.

The angry waves that lately broke
  High in the cliff, with loud, continuous roar,
Breathe out their lives in one last sob,
  And silence reigns along the peaceful shore.

Low in the sky, the setting sun
  Fills all the scene, e'er yet his glories pass,
Till, mirrored in the flood, we see
  The heavenly vision of the sea of glass.

We gaze beyond the glowing light
  Deep in the west, where sky and ocean meet,
And see, like him in Patmos isle,
  The pearly entrance and the golden street.

The forms of those we long since lost
  Bright with celestial glory then appear,
Each face reflecting perfect joy,
  For God has wiped away the mourner's tear.

We kneel upon the fading shore
  And stretch our eager hands to that dear home,
Where, safe within God's Paradise,
  We dread no more earth's storm nor billow's foam.

One trembling step, but He will guide
  Whose voice once bade the waves their raging cease,
And far above the spreading tide
  We enter God's eternal home of peace.

INDIAN SUMMER.

By Laura H. Feuling.

THE rainbow lights are on the woods,
    And all the hills infold,
And, far away, the solitudes
    Are lit with rays of gold,
The yellow leaves come drifting down,
    Soft as a cradle rhyme;
And so it was ere she was gone,
    Last year, this time!

The fields are gay with golden-rod,
    The sumach burns like flame:
And there the wild white asters nod.
    The very, very same.

A truant bird on yonder bough
  Calls like a matin chime;
'T was singing then as blithe as now —
  Last year, this time !

No strange bloom on the year is set,
  Unlike the beauty flown ;
And so I know He 'll not forget
  To give us back our own.
He gives the violet its blue,
  The year its sunlit prime :
He 'll keep for us the face we knew
  Last year, this time !

"SOMEBODY."

By May Kidder.

SOMEBODY lifted her curly head
  To her dear mamma's kind face, and said :
" You say that for me His blood was shed
  On the cross for my salvation ! "

Somebody knelt, with veiled head bent,
As the bishop came, the messenger sent
To give to souls the sacrament
  Of Holy Confirmation.

Somebody lifted her sweet young face
To that of the priest, as he tried to trace
In her tear-dimmed eyes, the blessed grace
  And strength of consolation.

Somebody knelt at the altar-rail,
With sad, calm face, so thin and pale,
And a look so holy, and yet so frail,
  To take the Cup of Salvation.

Somebody lay in her last repose,
In her dear, dead hand a half-blown rose,
And the voices were sad and low of those
    Who were left in desolation.

Somebody lies in the churchyard by,
And over her bends the clear, blue sky,
As the old bells seem to ring out the cry :
    "I am the Resurrection!"

SURSUM CORDA!

By M. E. Beauchamp (Filia Ecclesiae).

O SOUL, that hast a right to higher life,
    Why be content with this poor mundane sphere?
Forgetful of thy lofty heritage,
    Why should thy fears and wishes centre here?

Rise up, O heart, above this dark, cold sod,
    Rise into warmer air and purer light,
And see the petty joys and cares of earth
    Dwindle and vanish from thy soaring sight!

In thy brief absence from our Father's courts,
    Wilt thou forget thy lineage divine?
And more esteem the exile's mean array
    Than all the treasures that are truly thine?

Why should we love, and strive to make like home,
    This one-night lodging in a basement cell?
When the whole palace overhead is ours,
    And in its stately chambers we shall dwell.

Lift up your hearts!   Too long have we bestowed
    On this poor earth our being's noblest powers,
Lift up your hearts ! lift them to His abode,
    His who alone can fill these hearts of ours!

THE DOVE THAT RETURNED NO MORE.

By E. S.

WHEN o'er the plain one dreary waste of water
    Dashed its fierce spray above the forest tree,
How sweet the refuge, and how blest the shelter,
    Oh, weary dove, the ark held forth to thee!

But oh! the days of weary, sickening longing
    For air and sunshine, on thy flight to soar;
The thrill of rapture when, thy pinions spreading,
    Thou couldst fly forth in the glad Spring once more.

Alas! not yet thy captive days are over,
    Not yet thy home is in the mountain pine;
Back to thy refuge once again returning,
    Fold thy sad wing, and hope again resign.

It may not be, — again the eager flutter,
    The throbbing heart, the eye that begs release, —
Fly forth, dear bird, and bring, when evening closes,
    The leaf that tells of pardon and of peace.

Fly forth again, upon thy way rejoicing,
    In God's own sunshine, at thy pleasure soar;
The flood has ceased, the rainbow smiles triumphant,
    The dove, set free at length, returns no more!

O weary soul! O longing heart! a shelter
    Beneath God's altar thou art blest to find;
Canst thou not rest, in peace and safety dwelling,
    And all thy longings and thy quests resign?

It cannot be; the spirit's deathless craving,
    Nor rest, nor peace, alone can satisfy;
It must have freedom, storm and darkness braving,
    God gave the wing, 't is He that bids it fly.

In vain, again, and yet again, returning,
    It finds that earth for it has but one Home —
Yet from its flight one leaf of promise bringing,
    A moment's glimpse of happier days to come.

And they shall come, — the eager pinion, stretching
    In God's own sunshine, shall exult and soar:
Bursting the limits of its earthly prison
    The soul, set free at last, returns no more!

TIRED.

By Gertrude E. Heath.

DEAR Brother, I am tired: take my hand
      And lead me safely to thy Fatherland.
The path is stern and rough, my weary feet
Are torn and hot.   O Brother, sweet,
Canst Thou not comfort me?   I am so worn.
Thou dost not know the pain that I have borne.
Thou dost not know how oft I have sunk down
Beneath my heavy cross — how far the crown
Has seemed; and I have thought, O Brother, sweet.
There was no crown for me.   My tired feet
Refused to move.   And yet by some strange power
I have gained needed strength until this hour.

But now I am so tired!   I cannot rise.
Oh, bear me safely on to sunnier skies!
The way is dark, so dark I cannot see
One step before my feet, — oh, pity me!

I tried to rise; alas! I cannot move!
O Brother, raise me up by Thy dear love!
My dress is soiled and torn, its beauty gone —
Too poor for one like Thee to look upon.

I know I have been wrong, and lost my way.
Take, take my hand! No more from Thee I 'll stray.

Dear Brother! Oh, how kind to seek me out!
I should have perished quite, Thy care without.
Dear Saviour, take my hand! Hold, hold it tight!
Close-folded in Thine own, oh, happy night!
No more to walk alone, but close to Thee, —
White hands, and robe, and heart, Thy gift to me.

Ah! this is worth it all, — the thorny way,
The darkness, grief, and pain, each shadowed day.
For now I know that He, my Brother, sweet,
Walked with me all the way; and when my feet
Refused their task, 't was He that raised me up.
'T was he, my Brother dear, who filled each cup
That was my daily drink; and it is He
Whose hand is folding mine — who leadeth me!

MARY'S BIRTHDAY.

By P.

'TIS your birthday, my precious, my darling,
    Or would be if you were on earth;
I think it must still be your birthday,
    Though born to your heavenly birth.
The angels, I know, are as sweet
    As these lovely white roses I twine;
Their love may be pure and complete,
    But never more tender than mine.
Are you glad in their gladness, my darling?
    Do you laugh in their innocent glee?
Or are you lonely in Paradise,
    Waiting and wishing for me?

As I stand now and look at your picture.
  And drop on the roses my tears,
As I pray for the touch of your fingers
  To comfort my sorrows and fears ;
So light is the veil that 's between us,
  To the mother the child is so near,
The breath of my soul is suspended
  For your accents so tender and clear.
O my glorified darling, most precious,
  The one gift I thought was all mine !
I have lent you, not lost you, my darling,
  Only lent to the Love that 's divine.

There are moments so sweet and so solemn
  That my soul bursts its prison of pain,
And soars to the realm of the spirit,
  And meets my own darling again.
Then, calm from that saintly communion,
  I defy every foe of the world ;
I scorn every breath of contumely,
  Every shaft by its ignorance hurled.
Why these black robes of grief and of mourning
  Do I wear for a spirit like thee,
When my heart should be filled with thanksgiving
  That my child from sorrow is free ?

ALONE.

BY THE REV. NELSON AYRES.

I SLEPT, and dreamed a dream of light :
  I seemed to pass the ocean's foam.
To greet the southern sunshine bright,
The sparkling waters, land bedight
  With tropic blossoms : now I roam
No more ; but happy plight !
  Embrace my children and my wife at home.

Oh, happy dream! Oh, vision rare!
  This longing tension of my heart
Was gone. I sat all free from care,
And gazed upon that face so fair,
  That thrills my soul's most secret part,
And said, No fate shall tear
  Ever again our throbbing hearts apart.

I woke. The night was dark and cold.
  The chilly rain with sullen sound
Was pouring down. The thunder rolled
In hollow peals. A dread untold
  My heart in chains of sadness bound.
Alone, and unconsoled
  By light, and home, and love, myself I found.

Alas! how oft in waking hours
  We dream such dreams of love and joy:
Enraptured walk enchanted bowers;
Taste of love's fruits, and pluck her flowers!
  All happy bliss without alloy,
All peace and rest are ours;
  Nor heavy cares, nor shaking fears annoy.

But soon the harsher things of life
  Arouse us from the vision blest;
Its daily cares, its sordid strife,
Fierce jealousies, and rumors rife,
  Bring to the spirit deep unrest.
Alone and sad is life,
  By darkling storm and solitude opprest.

Alone must every spirit fare,
  E'en through the full world's crowded ways;
Yet not alone! For even there,
In stormiest night of trouble, prayer
  Will find a God, who ever stays,
With never-failing care,
  On His eternal staff, the soul that prays.

His love a shelter sure provides;
  He hears the sorrowing sufferer's moan;
Beneath His wings' broad shadow hides
The storm-beat soul; and gently guides
  To Him the lone and wandering one.
Whatever ill betides,
  Who rests on God is never left alone.

"HE GIVETH SNOW LIKE WOOL."

By I. W. P.

WHEN nature's biting northern blast
    Hath sealed the rills of water fast,
And all seem on God's mercies cast,
  " He giveth snow like wool."

When all around is bleak and drear,
And some grow faint, and many fear,
As winter's sterile form draws near,
  " He giveth snow like wool."

When precious seeds in furrows lie,
To human seeming like to die,
As the dread north wind passeth by,
  " He giveth snow like wool."

To clothe anew earth's naked form,
With mantle pure and fresh and warm,
And screen it from the raging storm,
  " He giveth snow like wool."

To symbolize the pure and true,
And show a nature rendered new, —
Which naught but heavenly grace can do, —
  " He giveth snow like wool."

THE SOUL'S LESSON.

By Mrs. J. D. H. Browne.

SO hard, so hard to learn !
  It has taken years upon years ;
For the teaching seemed hard and stern,
  And she could not see for tears.

So hard, so hard to learn !
  She longed for the lighter task ;
The poor weak heart would yearn,
  And the faltering lips would ask.

Ah, foolish heart, to seek
  For a smoother, easier road !
A way is made for the meek
  That will lead them straight to God.

So hard, so hard to learn !
  For the soul's eyes were too dim
With looking down, to discern
  That the rough ways lead to Him.

Laden with love and care, —
  Poor earthly care and love, —
Life had no room for the prayer
  That lifts to the peace above.

So hard, so hard to learn !
  By grief was the lesson taught,
Ere the thirsty soul could turn
  To the stream that faileth not, —

Ere the blinded soul could grope
  Towards the Light that can never fade,
Could taste of the deathless hope,
  Of the rest that Our Lord has made.

9

So hard, so hard to learn!
  And yet when learned how sweet
From earth and its griefs to turn,
  And lie at the Master's feet.

CHEER UP, FAINT HEART!

BY MRS. JANE M. MEAD.

CHEER up, faint heart!
  Plans never fail that are of God's designing.
  Weep not for glad days gone;
  No mourning garb put on;
Though storms roar loud, behind the cloud
The same bright sun is ever, ever shining.

Cheer up, faint heart!
Be brave, be brave; yield not to doubt nor sorrow.
  Hope's star may seem to set,
    And friends grow cold; but yet —
Be strong, be strong! Life is not long
The night is short; the sun will rise to-morrow.

Cheer up, faint heart!
Fear not the foe; the war will soon be over.
    Trust thou thy Leader's skill
    To rescue thee; He will.
O'er God's true child Heaven's wardens mild
Keep constant guard, and angel pinions hover.

Cheer up, faint heart!
Thy greatest fear needs be the fear of sinning.
    Adversity may come,
    And grief's keen darts strike home,
But trust Him still thy cup to fill
With joy, who knows the end from the beginning.

A YEAR IN PARADISE.

BY THE REV. JOSEPH CROSS, D.D., LL.D.

THE saddest days of all the year
 My saddest thoughts renew,
When Autumn winds with foliage sere
 The mount and meadow strew,
And midnight clouds are dark and drear,
 And stars are faint and few.

A year to-night since, far away,
 I paced the silent room,
And wailed the cold, impassive clay
 Apparelled for the tomb,
More mindful of its dark decay
 Than its reviving bloom.

But, oh! while oft, with aching eyes,
 I nightly vigils kept,
Why did not faith's strong pinions rise
 To where the saint I wept,
Secure from pain, in Paradise,
 On Jesu's bosom slept?

A year in Paradise! — How strange!
 What note is there of time,
What seasons of successive change,
 What tower's melodious chime,
What measure of the spirit's range,
 What bound to thought sublime?

A year in Paradise! — Released
 With victor's lute and palm,
A guest at God's eternal feast
 To swell the holy psalm,
The tempest of the passions ceased
 In love's celestial calm.

A year in Paradise! — How blest
　Is thy condition now!
New-born, by elder saints caressed,
　With bloom-encircled brow;
While I, an exile sore distressed,
　Beneath my burden bow.

A year in Paradise! — No tears
　In that fair land are known;
No gloomy doubts nor ghastly fears
　Their baleful seeds have sown;
No broken hearts through blighted years
　Sustain their griefs alone.

A year in Paradise! — Serene
　In fellowship made sure,
With spirits robed in goodly sheen,
　And fruit of faith mature,
Mid fields of never-fading green
　And living waters pure.

A year in Paradise! — Ah me!
　Who linger yet below,
Through weary days to weep for thee,
　And nights of deeper woe,
Till death shall set the captive free
　And bid me rise and go!

A year in Paradise! — But why
　Lament the dead that live
Where He who lives no more to die
　Will life eternal give,
And all who on His word rely
　The boon divine receive?

A year in Paradise! — And soon
　My spirit thine may trace,
Perchance before another moon,
　To meet thee face to face,
And bask in love's immortal noon
　With all the heirs of grace.

A year in Paradise ! — How sweet
   That precious hope to me !
Before the Saviour's throne to greet
   My other self in thee,
And bow to kiss the nail-pierced feet
   And bless the cursed tree !

A year in Paradise ! — Oh, rest
   Till that last gift be given ;
Till Christ return — the King confessed,
   And charnel houses riven
Shall roll their chant from east to west,
   And Paradise be Heaven !

BEYOND.

By Erastus C. Delavan.

TWO weary feet,
   Grown tired upon earth's thorny road,
      Have entered in
   The peaceful paradise of God.

Two loving eyes
   That looked her boy's heart through and through,
      And sweetly shared
   His burdens, that the mother knew. .

Two willing hands
   Are folded now, their work well done ;
      The way was long,
   And sweet the setting of life's sun.

An angel face
   From which the clouds of earth have fled —
      A radiant face !
   On which the Saviour's love is shed.

Why should we mourn?
    The way was long. the rest was sweet,
        And ere she went
    She walked with God with willing feet.

Oh! sainted one,
    Beneath our cross we struggle on,
        And hail the day
    That joins wife, father, sister, son.

"SHALL I NOT SEE THEM WAITING STAND?"

By Mrs. J. H. Meech.

LIFE'S greenest spots were quickly past,
    Life's brightest stars are sinking fast,
Yet have I you, and heaven, at last,
Dear friends, whose feet have gone before
To wait upon the eternal shore
For one with whom you walked of yore.

Between me and eternity
Life's darkest shadows seem to lie,
Like clouds against a summer's sky;
Swiftly I near the eternal strand;
Soon shall I reach the immortal land
There to rejoin my household band.

O dwellers in God's Paradise,
Looking on me with love-lit eyes
Out from your home beyond the skies!
I see your hands stretched forth to me;
Across the vast eternal sea
Your voices call incessantly.

Separate from me, on holier shore,
Your feet are set; tho' severed far,
Still in my heart I hold you more
Than all the loves of outlived years.
Above the din of earthly cares,
Thro' all the mist of blinding tears
I see your white hands beckon me;
Across the vast, eternal sea
Your voices call incessantly.

AT REST.

By Frances A. Shaw.

NOW God be praised she in His peace reposes, —
This gray-haired saint from all earth's woes at rest.
In the clasped hands, her emblems, June's sweet roses,
Its pure white lilies on her purer breast!

Tried, patient one! faithful to every duty,
Careful and anxious about many things,
Yet ever mindful that life's highest beauty
Lies in the service of the King of kings

The hand of Martha and the heart of Mary
In thee found union mystical and sweet;
Given to "much serving," ne'er of good works weary,
Thy chosen place was still at Jesus' feet.

O soul, that soared on ever joyous pinions,
With David's psalm, with Miriam's song of praise,
That found its home in Art's serene dominions,
Yet never scorned the lowliest household ways!

O spirit chastened in the school of anguish,
Doomed from life's earliest to its latest breath
To see hopes perish, fairest home-flowers languish,
And yield at last to the grim reaper Death!

O Niobe, ever loved and lost ones weeping,
Yet hiding from the world grief's wound and smart!
The *Mater dolorosa*, vigils keeping
O'er her Son's tomb, scarce bore a sadder heart.

Now dawns thy brighter day, thy compensation;
The cross so meekly borne at last laid down,
Thou comest up through earthly tribulation
Unto thy blood-washed robe, thy victor's crown.

Dear mother-heart, so brave and yet so tender,
Counting as naught love, labor, sacrifice,
The seed sown here in toil and tears, shall render
Sheaves golden and immortal in the skies!

"THY WILL BE DONE."

By the Rev. C. W. Leffingwell, D. D.

WE stood beside her little couch,
 With tearful eyes and struggling breath;
And vainly, in our wild despair,
  We strove with death.

In agony we prayed to God,
 "Oh, spare! oh, spare our little one!"
And then, by faith, we tried to say,
  "Thy will be done."

Our breaking hearts would scarce consent;
 Our quivering lips could scarce repeat;
At last we bowed submissively
  At Jesus' feet.

Then, as we watched, a heavenly light
 Beamed from her large and lustrous eyes,
Through which the soul serenely passed
  Beyond the skies.

We laid her wan and wasted form
  Beneath the whispering leaves to rest ;
The angels gently placed her soul
      On Jesus' breast.

Her little feet have never strayed —
  The paths of sin have never trod ;
Our precious lamb is safe within
      The fold of God.

We love her still, and fondly keep
  The little clothes she used to wear,
Her pretty playthings, and a lock
      Of silken hair.

We love her still with hallowed love,
  Refined and purified by grief —
By sorrow that alone in Faith
      Can find relief.

God help us in these darkened hours ;
  We cannot bear our grief alone ,
Help us, though stricken, still to say,
      " Thy will be done."

CHERITH.

By Katherine N. Ward.

FATHER ! Thy blessed hand, in love,
    Still guides my footsteps here,
And ever on my pilgrim way,
  Thy sheltering arm is near.

Tho' raven wings of sorrow cloud
  The skies above my head,
They bring a ministry of strength
  As from my daily bread.

As to Thy chosen one of old,
　They come with morning light,
And still at quiet eventide,
　Scarce vanish with the night.

Thy Cherith stream of blessing flows
　Yet day by day to me;
Nor will it fail until I stand
　Upon the glassy sea.

When in that hallowed land above,
　The sinless joys of heaven,
I drink the cup that ever flows,
　Redeeming love has given,

Then shall each lowly sorrow come
　In white-robed angel's guise,
That pointed here the pathway home
And led me to the skies.

A MOTHER'S LOGIC.

BY THE REV. FRANK N. WESTCOTT.

YOU are shocked at my strange confession
　Of an error, you say, that you dread,
That I for my boy should be praying,
　Even now, when I know he is dead.

I confess I 'm not skilful to answer
　In the old controversial art,
The only defence I can offer
　Is the logic that springs from the heart.

Suppose you had loved, with a passion
　That absorbed all your thoughts and your cares,
A boy that God placed in your keeping,
　To be blessed by your love and your prayers;

And then when he grew into manhood,
  Felt the touch of a sordid world's life,
And you knew the perils before him,
  That threatened his soul in the strife,

You prayed all the more in his danger
  That his heart might be kept pure and fair,
Till it seemed that each waking moment
  In its love was the breathing of prayer.

Suppose that the shadow of suffering
  Deepened suddenly over the day,
And your heart stood still in its anguish
  And you could do nothing but pray,

As you watched and felt all too surely,
  As the darkness grew deep in the night,
That everything dearest and truest
  Was departing far out of your sight.

And after it all was quite over,
  And they 'd taken his body away,
Then what would you do in your anguish
  That first night when you kneeled down to pray?

When you came to the place in your asking
  Where for years you had spoken his name,
Would you choke down the words in your sobbing,
  As if for the thought there were blame?

Is the God that you love so cruel
  To forbid you this comfort so dear?
If you yield to your heart's deep prompting
  Must you do it with doubting and fear?

Has his soul ceased to need God's protection, —
  Gone quite out of reach of God's care,
That there's nothing that God can give him
  In response to your heart-broken prayer?

He still waits with you his Lord's coming,
  Not yet is he perfectly blessed;
His soul must grow purer and stronger, —
  God can give him refreshment and rest.

Surely, then, you would pray for these blessings, —
  Your heart could not help it, I 'm sure;
And in sight of the God that made you,
  All your prayers would be blameless and pure.

And each earnest prayer that you uttered
  Would bring you more peace, if not joy,
And keep you in closer communion
  With your sweet-hearted, angel-faced boy.

And so had you loved him and lost him,
  You never could question your right;
You would kneel and ask God to bless him,
  As of old when you kissed him good-night.

A THOUGHT.

By A. V. R. S.

THERE is a thought whose coming
  Has often made me glad;
It drives away the lonely pain
  That makes my spirit sad.
This is the thought that soothes my pain:
In Heaven we can meet again.

When many bitter fears arise
  That I may never see
Again some dear, familiar face,
  Now far away from me, —
To hush my fears, soft swells the strain :
In Heaven we can meet again.

When thoughts that I could never reach,
　In case of need, the dying bed ;
That long ere I could gain the place
　They would be lying 'mong the dead ;
Still comes the noble, sweet refrain :
In Heaven we can meet again.

When longing for a tender word
　From some one passed away, —
Some love or some forgiveness breathed
　From now insensate clay, —
There 's promise in the soothing strain :
In Heaven we can meet again.

Oh ! blessed promise, full of cheer
　To yearning hearts below !
What blessedness to feel, to hope,
　What blessedness to know
That, though our loved are from us ta'en
In Heaven we can meet again.

Yes ! there we can our friends rejoin !
　Free choice to us is given,
Whether to say farewell for aye,
　Or, we will meet in Heaven.
Christ's blood can wash away each stain.
Through Him we meet in Heaven again.

Here must we strive to do His will,
　And thus our human love,
That once bound closely to the earth,
　Will draw us up above :
Blessings of parting will be plain
When up in Heaven we meet again.

And Father, when we praise Thy name
　For countless blessings here :
Or, when in some dark, lonely hour
　Slow falls the bitter tear,
Howe'er we feel, we 'll swell the strain ;
Thank God that we can meet again !

VIA SOLITARIA.

By Julia E. Phelps.

THE night comes on — the silent night —
  And storms have ceased, the valley sleepeth.
On forms beloved, far out of sight,
  My thought her solemn vigil keepeth.

With holy hush I walk the round,
  Remembered voices softly calling
My pilgrim feet to rest profound ;
  And chill with dew the night is falling.

Dear scenes ! where once my Eden bloomed;
  The fairest flowers so quickly gathered,
Storm-tossed and blighted, lie entombed,
  Cut down like grass, dried up and withered.

Now strangers walk those windings sweet
  Where sleep the loved ones, free from ills,
And other eyes with rapture greet
  The rosy dawn, the grand old hills.

So far, and yet so near they seem, —
  The greenwood groves, the shady dells,
The sunset glow, and in my dream
  Your holy chime, sweet Auburn bells !

I scarce could see, through tear-filled eyes,
  Ancestral homes and haunts forsaken.
On golden blooms in other skies
  I gaze, and happier thoughts awaken.

Though lost to mortal sight, I know
  They live again, in homes Elysian,
Where streams of living waters flow, —
  I see them still, oh, wondrous vision !

Then will I stand beside the loved,
  When time is not, and love an ocean,
All sin and striving far removed,
  And soul meets soul in rapt devotion, —

There walk with them the golden street
  With Him who Life Eternal giveth, —
Loved Jesus ! mine — oh, rapture sweet,
  To know that my Redeemer liveth !

"ASK AND IT SHALL BE GIVEN YOU."

By C. H. B.

" ASK what thou wilt ; it shall be done for thee,
    Each prayer is heard before My Throne above ;
No prayer is left unanswered, made to Me
    In holy fear and penitence and love."

" I know it, Lord ; yet I remember well
    The gifts I asked of Thee in early years ;
They are not mine, — their joys I cannot tell, —
    For there is nought, save pain, and grief, and tears."

" Didst thou, my child, pray for them in My Name,
    Obedient to the Father's holy will ?
Or didst thou — thought of sorrow deep, and shame —
    Seek God's sweet gifts for thine own pleasures still ?

" The prayer is thine — the answer is Mine own ;
    It ever comes on wings of mercy sent,
Wrapt in the cross that daily weighs thee down,
    Folded within life's blessings to thee lent.

" Be strong, and patiently await My will!
   Thy prayers shall find a home within My heart;
Be faithful unto death, that I may fill
   Thy soul with joys which never shall depart."

" Do what Thou wilt, it shall be well for me;
   I give myself to Thine eternal love.
Grant to me, Lord, in Thy good time to see
   The answer to my prayers in realms above."

THE LAST SLUMBER.

By Edwin B. Russell.

THE summer day in gradual close,
   Sank o'er the hills in purple rest,
And glimmered in its soft repose,
   Through all the peaceful west.
She slept! the quiet evening breeze
Had lulled her soul in gentle ease.

She woke not as an old refrain
   Was sung by one who loved her well;
The murmurs of a sweeter strain
   Upon her seemed to dwell, —
Far echoes in the soul, to keep
Her sorrows hush'd to heavenly sleep.

The stars through all the shining skies,
   Rose o'er the fading twilight gloom;
Yet still she slept, while troubled sighs
   Breathed sadness in that solemn room.
But she lay calm in blessed grace,
And made that room a holy place.

Yet darker grew the evening gloom,
  Still brighter shone the starry sky,
And on her face there came a bloom,
  As if an angel nigh
Had touched his harp, and o'er her flung
The magic of the song he sung.

She slept: the waves of moonlight filled
  Through all the heavens a flood of peace.
Softly the heart-beats paused and stilled —
  And yet more soft her soul's release.
Release and rest! nor joy nor pain
Shall wake her to the world again.

But sometimes in the light of stars
  We think we see her gentle smile;
And oft through music's golden bars
  We think we hear her voice awhile.
Where'er she is — what sea, what shore —
We know her blessed evermore!

Poems of Patience.

WAITING!

BY MAIE ALLYNE.

I STAND and wait at the beautiful gate,
  But it opens not for me,
While over its bars, 'mid the tender stars
  One bides, my sweet companie.

In this weary land, may I touch His hand,
  And feel His star's guiding ray,
Though I wait so long, through the pain grown strong
  I shall reach the shining way.

Then may I behold by the gleam of gold
  Why the cloud o'ershadows here,
And the Lord denies to my painéd eyes
  Glad use, in His service dear.

While to hold me still, if it be His will,
  With a loving heart and true,
Is a service meet, to the Lord as sweet
  As the love that hastes to do.

So I sing to my heart, and the song impart;
  'T is a sunbeam through ways dim,
Sometime I shall know, when the tide ebbs low,
  Somewhere will my love find Him.

SILENTIUM.

By David Melville.

I STAND and wait in shadow at His feet,
  The silence lies around me, pure and sweet,
And I am dumb and ready as is meet.

I know my Master sees me standing here;
So, though in gloom, I cannot let a fear
Enter my heart; for He is ever near.

Around me, and about me, and above,
The shield and shelter of His mighty love
Clings close, and will not ever let me rove.

I long, I pray a laborer to be,
I listen for His least command to me,
But still He wills it that I wait to see, —

Ready to toil or suffer for His sake,
But yet contented with this present state, —
" They also serve who only stand and wait."

Few tasks appointed fill my little day;
But I can let, through me, some tiny ray
From His true light illumine the dark way.

Perhaps in time the blest command will come
That sends me forth a guide to those who roam, —
To bring with loving care some wanderer home.

Meanwhile, dear Lord, give me Thy grace most sweet,
To wait with patience 'neath Thy mercy seat,
And fall in adoration at Thy feet!

Ready to do whatever is Thy will,
With praise to Thee some other life to fill,
Or, if 'tis best, to suffer and be still.

"HE LEADETH ME."

By M. E. PALMER.

IN pastures green? Not always; sometimes He
   Who knoweth best in kindness leadeth me
In weary ways, where heavy shadows be,

Out of the sunshine, warm and soft and bright,
Out of the sunshine into darkest night.
I oft should faint with sorrow and affright,

Only for this — I know he holds my hand;
So whether in a green or desert land
I trust, although I may not understand.

And by still waters? No, not always so:
Ofttimes the raging tempests round me blow,
And o'er my soul the waves and billows go.

But when the storm beats loudest, and I cry
Aloud for help, the Master standeth by
And whispers to my soul, "Lo! it is I."

Above the tempest wild I hear Him say;
"Beyond this darkness lies the perfect day;
In every path of thine I lead the way."

So whether on the hill-top high and fair
I dwell, or in the sunless valley where
The shadows lie — what matters? He is there.

And more than this; where'er the pathway lead,
He gives to me no helpless, broken reed,
But His own staff sufficient for my need.

So where He leadeth I can safely go;
And in the blest hereafter I shall know
Why, in His wisdom, He hath led me so.

NO LIFE FOR NAUGHT.

By E. S.

AN insect on the under side a leaf, —
   Its home, its world, that yet unnoticed falls
From some great tree that stretches wide its arms
   And to its shade the grateful cattle calls ;
Less than the least of worms like this am I,
Yet known and cared for by one watchful Eye.

Or stood that tree deep in some forest vast
   Where myriad leaves bud forth and live and die,
Then in the dust, in fragrant, billowy heaps,
   Trod by chance wayfarers, unnumbered lie ;
Such, Lord, am I, and yet my very dust
I know that Thou wilt keep, a sacred trust.

Perhaps the worm that lives its little day
   On that green leaf, a thread so fine may spin
That, wrought in some rich fabric, it may deck
   A queenly form, and words admiring win :
Even so Thy grace can take some word of mine,
And in Thy Bride's own raiment let it shine.

Perhaps from that forgotten, mouldering heap
   Some little seed, by bird or wild bee brought,
May spring up to some flower of beauty rare ;
   Then was that little leaf's short life for naught ?
So would I sleep forgotten in my grave,
While o'er my head such flowers of beauty wave.

A speck, a mote among unnumbered worlds
   And countless ranks of being, — such our lot.
What can we hope ?   Awhile our part to play,
   To weep, to laugh, then die and be forgot ;
Yet has each life its place, its work, its crown,
Its just reward, its endless, sure renown !

"EVEN AS THOU WILT."

BY F. BURGE GRISWOLD.

CAN God's sweet gifts to me,
        Dependent be
On my own wish and will?
Is it as I may choose,
        Or may refuse,
That Jesus will fulfil

My spirit with his grace,
        Or will efface
His image from my soul,
And either reign within,
        Or leave to sin
And Satan all control?

Oh! dreadful power of mine!
        Lord, I resign
My wish and will to thee,
So shall my soul aspire,
        With strong desire,
Thy holy child to be.

WAITING.

BY L. D. S.

AT Jesus' feet a young disciple fell,
    And poured forth his complaint: " O Lord, we know
Beyond what Thou dost will sin cannot go,
But it is hard to war with shades of hell
Thy shining presence would at once dispel;
It is *so* long to wait the end of woe!"

His guardian angel stood and whispered low,
" Thou hast thy task ; do that — all else is well ! "

He rose, and with a sigh the voice obeyed,
And all his soul bent to his task alone,
Unheeding how age followed youth's bright noon,
Until the angel came again and said :
" The Master calleth ; rise, thy task is done ! "
And then he cried, in wonder rapt : " So soon ? "

"HE LEADETH ME."

BY THE REV. E. B. RUSSELL.

UPON my chamber's pictured wall,
   Before my couch this text I see,
Where first and last mine eyes must fall,
    The blessed words —
    " *He leadeth me !* "

The dawn's bright rays the sentence show,
   That so may waking joyous be ;
At midnight in the firelight glow
    The shining words —
    He leadeth me !

It tells how all the day my Lord
   Lights all my paths, His will to see,
And when I sleep keeps watch and ward :
    The guardian words —
    He leadeth me !

In health, as happy moments fly
 . When the sweet chords of life agree,
Or when in pain or grief I sigh :
    The precious words —
    He leadeth me !

How dear the hand that wrought this text
  In love, that I might daily see,
If joyful, sad, serene, perplext,
    The tender words —
    He leadeth me !

Be it the motto of my life,
  In mart or field, on land or sea :
My conquering song in death's dread strife,
    Triumphant words —
    He leadeth me !

IN THE PRINTING OFFICE.

By J. C. S.

"I CANNOT read it, Father ; Father, see !
  I cannot read it, spell it out for me ;
I thought that surely I my letters knew,
But this I find I really cannot do."

So spake a child who at his father's side
Walked through a printing room and vainly tried
To read the type.   The printer smiling laid
Upon the press a sheet, and kindly said,
" Come, little one, and try to read once more
These letters, for they were reversed before
But now they 're plain."   The clouds from that fair brow
Have passed away, for he can read it now.

So with our Father's dealings.   Day by day
We try to read, and puzzled turn away.
We do not understand, we cannot see
Why this was done, or that allowed to be.
But in the world to come, through His clear light,
We too shall read the mystery aright.

THE SCULPTOR.

By A. B. P.

'TIS the Master who holds the mallet,
  And day by day
He is chipping whate'er environs
  The form, away;
Which, under His skilful cutting,
  He means shall be
Wrought silently out to beauty
  Of such degree
Of faultless and full perfection
  That angel eyes
Shall look on the finished labor
  With new surprise,
That even His boundless patience
  Could grave His own
Features upon such fractured
  And stubborn stone.

'T is the Master who holds the chisel;
  He knows just where
Its edge should be driven sharpest,
  To fashion there
The semblance that He is carving;
  Nor will He let
One delicate stroke too many,
  Or few, be set
On forehead or cheek, where only
  He sees how all
Is tending — and where the hardest
  The blow should fall,
Which crumbles away whatever
  Surperfluous line
Would hinder His hand from making
  The work divine.

With tools of Thy choosing, Master,
  I pray Thee, then,
Strike just as Thou wilt, as often,
  And where, and when,
The vehement stroke is needed;
  I will not mind,
If only the clipping chisel
  Shall leave behind
Such marks of the wondrous working,
  And loving skill,
Clear carven in aspect, stature,
  And face, as will,
When discipline's hands are over,
  Have all sufficed
To mould me into the likeness
  And form of Christ.

MY STRENGTH AND I.

By Frances M. Buchan.

MY strength and I were boastful
  O'er the evil that might come;
We had worked together bravely
  Through tempest, shadow, sun.

The heights that towered above us
  We scorned as trivial things;
We made the ascent, fearless,
  For the triumph that it brings.

My strength and I knew nothing
  But endurance brave and strong;
We smiled when others fainted,
  Though the way seemed drear and long.

We thought this, consecration —
  My silly strength and I ;
Deemed it the Master's calling,
  For which we 'd dare to die.

A human pride did flatter
  My foolish strength and me ;
The grace and faith that quicken,
  Our blindness could not see.

A storm then fell about us,
  A whirlwind from the sky ;
We fought and struggled with it,
  My own proud strength and I.

A bitter, bitter contest,
  A friendship lying dead ;
My strength and I did bury
  That whence the soul had fled.

My strength and I drew closer
  And vowed we 'd never part, —
We were so true and trusting
  In word and deed and heart.

Then came a fear, so sudden
  Our very soul did quake ;
My strength and I did tremble
  O'er the havoc it did make.

And burden after burden
  Fell on my strength and me,
Till at last we staggered blindly
  With a load of misery.

Prostrate we fell, and waited, —
  No human aid had we ;
The Master's voice did call us —
  My shattered strength and me.

His loving Hand did raise us,
  He gave us power to see;
Thy grace, O God, can succor —
  We owe our strength to Thee.

Now is the truth made manifest
  To my humbled strength and me ;
At our Master's feet low kneeling,
  His strength in all we see.

The cross 'neath which we stumbled
  Has raised us up anew,
We pray, my chastened strength and I,
  For grace His work to do.

Legendary and Allegorical Poems.

---•---

A CHRISTMAS LEGEND.

By L. D. S.

IN years gone by, e'er man had seen
  A cross-capped spire, or heard a bell
  Its Christmas benediction tell,
When Force was king and Pride was queen,

Three captives in a dungeon lay,
  Each in a lonely cell confined,
  Bound hand and foot, chained heart and mind,
Shut out from hope and life and day.

A dark-skinned man from tropic skies,
  Whose sweat-damp brow was overhung
  By matted locks, that round it clung
Above the gleam of sullen eyes, —

This was the first: the stones his bed;
  For gems, steel bands 'round hands and feet;
  The rumble of the busy street
For lullaby above his head.

Strange the next cell!   A woman there
  As graceful as young alders are,
  Pale as the moon, each eye a star
Gleaming beneath her dusky hair.

And yet those eyes are dim with tears!
  And see! — they fall on chains of gold!
  Those gorgeous draperies enfold
A heart of woe, a breast of fears.

The third, — the last and worst of wrongs! —
  A little child, with garments torn,
  And face with care too early worn,
His feet confined with silken thongs.

Thus lay these captives many a year,
  Nor looked for succor save from death,
  When on a day with bated breath
They heard an unknown step draw near, —

A gentle step, as maid or boy,
  Yet firm, as one who for the right
  Goes forth into the deadly fight, —
A crown, a grave, were equal joy.

The first strong door flew open wide:
  The Fettered saw before his face
  One full of glory and of grace,
As childhood were it deified.

"Be free, O brother!"   From his hands
  And feet fell off the smitten steel;
  "Henceforth Love's dear constraining feel.
And joy to serve where He commands."

Again before that beauteous Child
　The fast-barred door swung open wide,
　And hastening to the woman's side,
He looked into her face and smiled.

" Who called thee *Eve* and bound thee here
　As *Mary* every tongue shall bless.
　Mother " (with infinite tenderness),
" Love perfected shall cast out fear."

His hand her golden fetters clave :
　She rose, and with an angel's look,
　Her draperies and ointment took,
And bound the chain-wounds of the slave.

With smile of deepest love and joy
　The Child threw wide the last barred door,
　And, filled with holy anger, tore
The thongs from off the fettered boy.

The slave, at Love's unvoiced behest,
　Lifted and gave the little one
　Into the woman's arms.　" My son ! "
She cried, and clasped him to her breast.

From thence into the light of morn
　The freed ones — now but three — outpassed.
　Bells pealed.　" What is this joy ? " they asked.
Men stared.　" Whence came ye ?　Christ is born ! "

A LEGEND OF SAINT AUGUSTINE.

By Mary Bayard Clarke.

WITH study spent and worn with care
　　A· bishop wandered by the sea,
A reverend Father of the Church,
　And skilled in its disputes, was he.

11

Long had he sought to know that truth
  Whose height no human mind can reach,
And earnest prayed for light divine
  On what he should and should not teach.

What was that God-Head over which
  The subtle Greek in keen debate,
Had wrangled until Christian love
  Seemed almost quenched in deadly hate?

As wrapped in thought he slowly walked,
  Scarce conscious of the evening breeze,
Upon the great sea's sandy beach,
  A little child at play he sees.

"What dost thou, little one?" he said,
  As with a conch-shell in each hand,
The child bore water from the sea
  To fill a hole scooped in the sand.

"Just what you vainly strive to do,"
  With solemn look the child replied;
"I seek to drain the ocean dry
  To fill a hollow by its side.

"As well do this as try to crowd
  Infinite truth in finite mind,
Or with your puny human powers
  The secret things of God to find."

Startled to hear from childish lips
  A truth so pointed yet so grand,
The bishop bowed his head and cried,
  "Before Thee, Lord, rebuked I stand."

But when he raised his eyes and saw
  The child had vanished from the beach,
He felt it was an angel sent,
  This mighty truth to him to teach.

THE LEGEND OF SAINT DOROTHEA.

(Inscribed to Flower Missions.)

BY KATHARINE READ LOCKWOOD.

FAIR Dorothy went up and down
The lanes and by-ways of the town,
God's peace upon her gentle brow,
God's peace within her heart, I trow, —
A maid whose every thought was given
To deeds of love and hopes of heaven.

Her life was made of sweet content:
On charity's kind errands sent
To souls that hungered, souls in pain,
To souls that doubted, souls in chain ;
Where ways were dark and men were fearing,
This lovely lady came with cheering.

The cross, Christ's symbol now world-wide,
A few brave hearts owned then aside.
The few brave hearts that bore His Name
Acknowledged Him through scoff and shame :
Fair Dorothy of these, — not hiding
Her Lord's reproach for foe's deriding.

One day a tumult rose in Rome,
Where Dorothea had her home.
" Seize all the Christians ! " was the cry, —
" Let not one Nazarene go by !
Ransack all corners of the city !
And burn them without show of pity."

Fair Dorothea with the rest
Was borne upon the crowd abreast.
Calm, pitiful, crossed by no doubt,
To Christ the Lord her heart went out.
What were her brief and fleeting losses
To His and all the martyrs' crosses ?

A youth, attracted by the stir,
" Ho, Dorothy!" called out to her
(Speaking within his palace door),
" You've had your way.   What ask you more?
You would not listen to my warning,
And so you die this dreadful morning.

" I could have saved you had we wed.
A broken reed, when all is said,
Is this Jew-god on whom you lean!"
She smiled, blue-eyed, gold-haired, serene.
" Nay," said she, without fail or falter;
" My sole Love waits me at the altar."

" You rave, you rave!   You throw aside
Life, beauty, wealth, and youth!" he cried.
" I go to Life more fair by far
Than any dreams of mortal are.
This night I shall behold the flowers
That bloom in Paradise's bowers."

" Oh, flowers!" he scoffed; " oh, Paradise!
You cheat yourself with fool's device;
And yet I love you.   This right arm
Would even yet shield you from harm.
Only recant!"   "And miss the blessing
That follows on a good confessing?

" Oh, slow of heart!   Why doubt you this?
Nay, when my soul hath gained her bliss,
I 'll pray some roses from the Warden
Of the immortal, heavenly garden;
I 'll send them to you as a token
That true are all the words I 've spoken."

She bowed her head, smiled, passed to death,
Praising her God with latest breath;
And many mourned her in the town
Where she went kindly up and down;
And one man, plunged in wild excess,
Could but lament her none the less.

That night a knock came at his door :
He opened it, and stood before
A boy with seraph brow and eyes,
Who, facing his confused surprise,
Held him fair boughs with roses laden, —
Gifts from the blessed Martyr Maiden.

Next day a rumor rang along
The wondering city's busy throng, —
Saint Dorothea's lover came
To those baptizing in Christ's Name !
" I do repent ! " he cried.   " Believe me,
And as Theophilus receive me."

Thus Theophile and Dorothy
(God's gift, God's love) in mystery
Of Baptism united were ;
And he became a minister
Of the young Church, and fondly cherished
Her Faith until for it he perished.

So runs her legend, fair and wise,
Who roses sent from Paradise ;
And in her name the Church since then
Sends flowers forth to suffering men, —
Such as she toiled among when living.
Sweet hints of heavenly comfort giving.

DOMINE, QUO VADIS?

(A Legend of Saint Peter.)

By Mary Bayard Clarke.

IN the dark days of Nero's reign,
   Whose hand with Christian blood was red,
Trembling before the heathen's rage,
From Rome, Saint Peter faithless fled.

'T was night; and through the city gate,
Where drunken guards in silence slept,
  No angel walking by him now,
With stealthy step he slowly crept.

  Fear paralyzed his soul, until
The dangerous spot was safely past,
  When conscience raised her voice and spoke
Those words his Lord had uttered last.

  Bowed down with shame, Saint Peter walked,
Till in the twilight dim and gray,
  He saw a well-remembered Form
Pass slowly down the Appian way.

  " Lord, whither goest Thou?" he cried,
And marked the cross the Saviour bore ;
  " I go to Rome," his Master said,
" There to be crucified once more."

  Saint Peter could not meet that glance
Of pitying love and deep reproof,
  Seen once, and only once before,
When from his Lord he held aloof.

  O'ercome with mingled grief and shame.
He fell in anguish on his knees,
  As gliding slowly on to Rome,
His Master's fading Form he sees

  It was enough ! in his grand soul
All fear and shame forever died ;
  Backward he turned, and nobly wrought,
Till he at Rome was crucified.

  And still, beside the Appian way,
The mark of Jesus' feet is shown ;
  But, ah ! its living print remains
In human hearts, and not on stone.

"DE IMITATIONE CHRISTI."

By Harriet W. French.

It is told of Thomas à Kempis that as he walked with his brethren in cloister and garden, he often withdrew from them, saying, " Dear Brethren, I must go ; One is waiting for me in my cell." What the voice of the Beloved said to Thomas and what the voice of the Disciple replied, we find in the wonderful treatise treasured in the devotion of centuries, — the treatise " Concerning the Following of Christ."

THROUGH the wide garden do the brethren pace,
 Where fall of fountains cools the crystal air
And birds sing sinless antiphon to prayer,
And flowers breathe fragrant incense through the place.

The brethren's hours of silence duly spent,
Now, in familiar speech of things around,
Of skies o'erhead and small blooms on the ground,
They take their harmless pleasure, full content.

For they who loftiest soar in heavenward flight,
Find the earth fair, and with a child's meek heart,
In lowly things learn God's dear love and art,
And, pure of spirit, win divinest sight ;

Joying in common charms of earth and sky,
In every varying hue of pulsing light,
In blushing rose, or lilies' mystic white,
And wood-note wild by breezes borne anigh.

So when from prayer and toil the brethren cease,
Cheerful, their cares they lay aside awhile, —
Freely go forth to bask in Nature's smile,
And take her gentle benison of peace.

In groups they stroll adown their 'customed walk,
And one, whose voice thrills with a tender joy,
As though some happy secret did employ
His deepest thought, beneath his lighter talk,

Says, simply, to his brethren standing near,
" Dear friends, I go ; ONE waits me in my cell."
And they, this Heavenly Favor knowing well,
List, half in hope the Voice Divine to hear.

What spake the Voice, and what the low return
Of the Disciple's earnest, meek reply,
In holy interchange and converse high,
They know whose hearts with love of Jesus burn,

In pondering o'er the sweet, grave words which tell
Of following Him whose voice bids us aside,
Wondrously willing with us to abide,
Awaiting each, in his own heart's deep cell.

BROTHER PHILIP.

By Harriet W. French.

L OFTY the walls of stone, stern, strong. and gray.
Where live, of earthly life and love forgot,
Marking with toil and chant each peaceful day,
The pious Brethren of the Common Lot.

Among them, on his menial tasks intent,
Patient to bear and do in daily round
Each smallest duty, Brother Philip went —
In hardest labor, chief contentment found.

To others. in their penance or their praise,
Were granted glimpses of the Life above,
Visions of bliss repentant souls to raise
To Him whose Being and whose Name is Love.

Never to *Philip* — counting weary years,
All vain, his penances, his prayers, he deemed.
   Borne down and broken by his weight of fears,
Of comfort, hope, or Heaven he hardly dreamed.

   Prone on the stony floor at dawn he lay,
Pouring his heart out in one fervent prayer
   For patience to abide his Lord's delay,
Lest faith should yield to sickening despair.

   " I am so weak," he cried, " so frail and fond,
My sins have hid from me Thy Blessed Face !
   I cannot soar these fleshly bounds beyond,
To feel the warmth and glory of Thy Grace.

   " How have I longed for Thee, my God, my Light,
And wearied heart and flesh in sleepless pain,
   Hoping, in torturing vigils of the night,
Thou wouldst draw near and call me by my name.

   " Dead even to God — forgotten in my cell,
How dare I hope the Beauteous King to see,
   When saints alone — alas ! I know full well,
Gain the blessed vision aye withheld from me ? "

   A sudden glory thrilled the ambient air ;
Warmth, fragrance, stillness filling all the space ;
   In midst, a radiant Form, Divinely fair,
And, sweet through suffering, smiled the Saviour's face.

   Quick, Philip stretched forth worn and wasted hands,
The raptured silence by no breath he broke,
   Waited Love's sweet, compulsory demands —
Alas ! no voice the trancéd hush awoke.

   But with imperious call clangs forth the bell,
The poor are gathered at the Convent gate ;
   Why comes not Brother Philip from his cell,
To dole the daily food for which they wait?

He *cannot* go — What ! leave his gracious Guest,
So long awaited, sought with anguished cry,
  When years may lapse e'er, all his fears at rest,
Death sets him free to see his Lord on high?

Again the walls give back the bell's deep tone,
And angry sounds of mingled voices rise ;
  A lull — and Philip hears a child's weak moan —
Then Famine's outcry, drowning women's sighs.

One instant lingered he upon his knees,
Recalling that his Master once had said,
  "To Me is done whate'er is done to these,"
Then forth to feed his Master's poor, he sped.

His sacred labor ended, back he hied,
To kneel within his late transfigured room,
  When lo ! even yet the place is glorified,
All richly glowing as a rose in bloom.

"Philip, Beloved, faithful in thy place !
Hadst thou remained and left My poor unfed,
  In selfish hope of more exceeding grace,
Leaving thee all unblest I must have fled."

So spake our Lord, in tones of tender calm,
And raised o'er Philip's head Hands beaming light, —
  Dear piercéd Hands, whose wounding is our balm, —
Then passed, in act of benison, from sight.

SAINT VERONICA.

By the Rev. Melville K. Bailey.

WEEPING she stood in that sad street
  Where, in morn's twilight gray,
Passed murmuring the saddest throng
  That saw earth's saddest day.

" O mournful lady, what hast thou,
   And wherefore dost thou weep,
And why do thy tear-laden eyes
   So long their vigils keep ? "

" I weep for Him ye bear away.
   Oh, lay this kerchief now
With tender touch upon the drops
   That stain His sinless brow ! "

They laid her kerchief on His face :
   Soft fell its folds, I ween,
On brow and eyes and grieving mouth,
   Where'er love's mark was seen.

And when they gave it back to her, —
   Oh, marvel strange to tell ! —
It bore the image of His face
   Who loved our race so well.

Then bear His body to the cross,
   Or bear it to the tomb,
Or let its living glory rise
   From low earth's twilight gloom ;

Yet this true lady hath the pledge,
   The seal of love and life, —
Of love for earth ; of life when death
   Makes peace of deathful strife.

And when the night drew down in shade,
   I think that she might see
The Face that lived in that soft veil
   Sad with Gethsemane ;

Or when the golden sunlight glowed
   In all its sacred folds,
It shone with that unconquered Life
   No rocky chamber holds ;

Or when a breeze stirred all the threads,
  Would pass a mystic grace,
Tender with pity and with love,
  Upon the wondrous Face.

And if it be not still at Rome,
  In Milan, or in Spain,
Yet is the tale not all untrue,
  Nor told us all in vain :

For all the world is but a veil
  Laid o'er Christ's living Face, —
In all its threads. and all its folds,
  His likeness we may trace.

His Image lives in earth's wide fields ;
  It trembles on the sea :
'T is joyous in the day's bright glow,
  Sad in night's mystery.

It is to us the faithful pledge,
  The seal of love and life, —
Of love for earth : of life when death
  Makes peace of deathful strife.

A MANSION IN HEAVEN.

(A Legend of Saint Thomas, Bishop of Abyssinia.)

BY MARY BAYARD CLARKE.

HIGH in the favor of the king.
  Thomas the Apostle stood :
Bishop of Abyssinia he,
  Whose title was " the Good."

" I trust this Christian," said the king ;
    " And in my absence he
Shall with my gathered treasures build
    A palace grand for me."

And then his treasury keys he gave
    Into Saint Thomas' hand :
" Two years I take my journey far,
    And leave thee in command.

" Build thou for me a palace fair, —
    Fairer than any known.
Thyself inspect each joist and beam,
    And lay the corner-stone."

He said, and on his journey went.
    Saint Thomas oped the door,
And daily from the treasury took
    Money to feed the poor.

And in the monarch's name he gave
    Outside the Church a dole ;
While he within prayed God that Christ
    Would turn the heathen's soul.

The years pass by : the king returns
    His palace to inspect,
And finding none, in prison threw
    The recreant architect.

" I 'll torture thee till back I get
    The treasures thou hast spent."
Without an answering word, the saint
    To prison calmly went.

That night, while in the prison bound
    Saint Thomas praying waits,
In sleep the angel took the king
    Up to the Golden Gates.

" Look in, O mighty king ! " he said :
  " Thy stately palace see !
'T was with thy treasures built by prayer
  In Paradise for thee.

" Eternal, and not made with hands,
  Where neither moth nor rust
Can fret that treasure or consume,
  Saint Thomas stored thy trust.

" Its stones are alms he daily gave
  From death to save thy soul,
And earnest prayer the cement which
  Consolidates the whole."

In awe the Abyssinian king
  Before the angel bowed,
And in the trouble of his soul
  In sleep he cried aloud.

Trembling he woke, and straight arose,
  And to the prison went,
And at the Apostle's feet so low
  His kingly head he bent.

" Teach me," he said, " that so I may
  Dwell in that mansion fair
Which thou hast built in Paradise
  For me by alms and prayer."

With his own hands he loosed the bonds,
  And led the saint away,
Who in his church baptized the king
  And all his house next day.

LAW AND LOVE.

By L. D. S.

I GAVE to Law a task to do —
    A morning journeying to take —
And whispered softly: " For my sake ! "
    As sadly from his playmates he withdrew.

    Across his features fell the shade,
And with no parting kiss he went ;
I stood and marked his discontent, —
    Stood saddened — yet he had not disobeyed.

    I gave to Love a task to do —
A far-off journey in the night ;
Her upturned face grew strangely bright,
    Her parted lips smiled back, " Oh, yes, for you ! "

    Not even did her singing cease,
As quickly she rose up from play,
And with a soft kiss sped away,
    And left my eyes all tears — my heart all peace.

THE MISTLETOE.

By the Rev. C. S. Percival, Ph.D.

WHEN summer is green 'mid the shadowing trees,
    Where fondly the mistletoe clings,
The passer perhaps in the verdure ne'er sees
    What they hide with their sheltering wings.
        It may flourish unseen
        'Mid the wide-spreading green
    Of the fostering bough where it springs.

But the autumn comes forth on his mission of death
  To revel in summer's bright realm, —
To scatter the leaves with his pitiless breath
  And the pride of the forest o'erwhelm :
      Then the mistletoe green
      In its beauty is seen,
  Clinging true to its desolate elm.

And then 't is a joy in their beauty to see
  Its tiny white blossoms appear,
Which ripen to fruit while the fostering tree
  In winter is naked and sere.
      Thus the mistletoe green,
      In the summer unseen,
  Findeth life in the death of the year.

And thus in a heart that is noble and true
  The rarest of virtues may dwell
In the time of prosperity, hidden from view
  By that which adorneth it well ;
      They may flourish unseen,
      Like the mistletoe green
  When summer is clothing the dell.

But when the chill winds of adversity blow,
  And the pleasure that earth can impart,
Like verdure autumnal, is shrouded in woe,
  Those virtues that never depart,
      Like the mistletoe green
      In the autumn, are seen
  Clinging true to that desolate heart.

When Fortitude, Patience, and heavenly Faith
  In lustre undying appear,
And life-giving Hope, sweetly smiling on Death,
  Points up to a holier sphere,
      Like the mistletoe green,
      All their beauty is seen
  When the winter of life draweth near.

THE MERCIFUL SCRIBES.

BY FLAVEL S. MINES.

AROUND them, so the Moslems say,
Two angels guard by night and day
To keep all evil thought away ;
And if a sinful deed is done,
Before the setting of the sun,
Or, e'er they lay them down to sleep —
He who the daily sins doth keep
Forbears to write, that for the sin
The doer may crave grace within.
And if the mortal doth repent
Before the appointed time is spent,
Estig fourillah (God pardons) then
Is the only record of his pen.

And he who standeth on the right
Doth all their better deeds indite
Before they can be lost to sight ;
And if there comes a goodly thought,
Or action blest by them is wrought,
At once, the angel on the scroll
Of Life, the record doth enroll ;
Hoping that if death should fall
Upon them unawares, o'er all
The goodness would predominate,
And earn for them the joys elate
Of that life with pleasures laden, —
The fair land, *Jannat al Aden.*

12

TREASURE.

By Flora L. Stanfield.

SADLY the rich man pondered : " How can I.
Knowing beyond all doubt that I must die.
Gather my wealth together in my hand,
So that, awaking in a fairer land,
It will be there to greet celestial sight ?
Let skilful lapidaries bring the light
Of all their jewels to me ! "   And he chose
A brilliant diamond, cut like a rose
And worth a monarch's ransom.   So he died
And in God's time awoke, and loudly cried :
" Where is my treasure ?   It was safe to-day ;
I must have lost it somewhere on the way."
" Be comforted ! " up spoke a shining one, —
" Your treasure is intact ; each good deed done.
Each penny given from your simple hoard
When you had little, every struggle toward
The heights the blessed reach, — all, all are here."
" But my lost diamond ! "   " I surely fear,"
Said the stern angel, " that the bit of dross
You call a diamond will prove a loss
Beyond retrieval."   Then the rich man sighed
And turned away, but suddenly espied
A tiny globe of light.   " Ah, here ! " he said,
" Here is my jewel ! " and a glory spread
Over his visage, but the angel smiled.
" That is the tear-drop of a starving child
To whom you ministered ; a banished tear
Is called a diamond by dwellers here."

THE MESSENGER OF PEACE.

By L. L. Robinson.

IN legends old — or dreams — I scarce can tell,
But somewhere in the realm where memories dwell,
I've heard the story told, how long ago
The mighty sea, wild with some hidden woe,
Beat its great breast, and tossing on its bed,
Shook with deep sobs that filled the earth with dread.
God's eye beheld ; the conflict sore and long
Touched His great love, and moved by pity strong
Gently He dropped within the seething whirl,
From His own Throne, a pure and priceless pearl.
Softly it fell, and lo ! with sudden thrill,
Through all the sea there breathed a " Peace, be still ! "

And thus I think it was at Christmas-tide,
When, torn with sin and baffled human pride,
Moaning in wild and unavailing pain,
Tossing in struggles endless, sore and vain,
Hopeless and worn with its unequal strife,
A vast, despairing sea, lay human life.
Then deep within this restless, seething whirl,
Thy Life was cast, O Christ, a priceless Pearl,
Down from the Father's Hand and Thy own Throne,
Laden with balm which Thou, and Thou alone
Could'st bring — Thou cam'st, and lo ! with deepening
thrill,
O'er all the sea there fell a " Peace, be still ! "

THE SERMON OF THE ROSE.

By Mary Livingston

WEARY with study and oppressed with care,
  One of earth's children sank in deep despair
Upon a mossy bank where sweetly grew
Some fragrant roses of the loveliest hue.

And there within the cool, sequestered shade
He wept, as all his life work he surveyed,
How every thought had been for other's good,
Yet thoughts and deeds had been misunderstood.

The seed that he had scattered o'er the land,
If grown, still brought no harvest to his hand;
The end of all was sorrow and regret,
And grief weighed down his eyelids, and he slept.

The sun went down, the night wind's gentle sigh
Breathed o'er the dreamer as it wandered by;
A red rose bent its shining petals near,
And softly whispered in the dreamer's ear:

" Oh, foolish man ! why thus lament thy lot?
The rose, too, shares it and yet grieveth not,
But gives its fragrance to the summer air,
Nor asks one blessing of the world so fair;

"Content, indeed, if in some lonely hour
It touched one heart with its unconscious power;
For sunshine, rain, and dew, alike on all
In tenderness upon earth's children fall."

The dreamer moved, a shower of petals fell
Upon his face, yet deep that silent spell;
And all the sweet rose said ere she was spent
Sank in his heart and he arose content.

WAITING.

BY E. A. CLARKE.

HE stood in the golden glory
  Of the early morning light,
While away in the dim, far distance
  Lay the fields for the harvest white.

With eager heart he had waited
  As his comrades were called away,
And he whispered, "Surely, the Master
  Will call me also to-day!"

But the soft bright tints of the morning
  Grew pale in the glowing sky,
And the sunbeams' burning kisses
  Left the leaves and the flowers dry.

To him there was sent no message,
  Though he waited, as oft before,
While others went forth to garner
  The harvest's bountiful store.

At length, when the falling shadows
  Told the close of the weary day,
He followed the last, who left him
  Weeping along the way.

And the messenger, turning backward
  Ere he entered the open gate,
Said, with sweetest look and accent,
  "'T is the Master who bids thee wait!"

They were not the words he had longed for,
  But he bowed to the Master's will,
And with downcast eyes turned homeward,
  Searching their meaning still.

As slowly he walked, beside him,
  Growing close to the busy street,
A lily he saw, dust-sprinkled
  And trampled by careless feet.

With a feeling of tender pity,
  He knelt by the fragile thing,
Its parched leaves bathed with water
  Pure and cold from a wayside spring.

And all through the harvest season
  He watched it with loving care,
Till at last a pure white blossom
  Crowned it with beauty rare.

And he knelt with the happy reapers,
  All bringing their sheaves complete,
With bowed head placing his lily
  Low at the Master's feet.

And then there arose a murmur
  As the reapers about him pressed :
He raised his eyes, the fair blossom
  Was placed on the Saviour's breast !

DISCORDS.

By Flora L. Stanfield.

A N earnest pupil, wearily intent
      Upon the measures of a little song;
A patient teacher, with dim vision bent
    Upon the slender hands that move along,
Interpreting vagaries which were born
In a musician's heart one happy morn.

"Songs Without Words" upon the printed page
    Speak of the master dear beyond compare ;
Songs without words, like wild birds in a cage,
    Flutter and fall upon the drowsy air ;
The reason why the teacher's sight is dim
Is that one day such songs were sung to him.

A tiny frown upon the pupil's brow,
    A crash upon the old piano's keys ;
" There is none wise enough to tell me how
    To find the harmony in chords like these :
Poor Mendelssohn was surely half insane
To spoil with faulty tones so fine a strain ! "

" My child," the teacher answered, " 't is the ears
    We listen with that makes the music sweet ;
He with untutored senses never hears
    The tones which make the melody complete.
This rule remember for your future good :
Grand harmonies are discords understood."

Our lives, like measures of the master's song,
    Have jarring notes, at which we, too, exclaim,
" God did not fashion sounds so wildly wrong
    As are these discords, and He will not blame
The one who sees no possible design
In such a wasted life as this of mine."

We tread a flinty path and cannot find
    The beauty in the mystery of pain ;
Perchance the dust of labor makes us blind,
    We miss the road and find it not again ;
And when the angels tell us of the way,
We murmur, " Discord ! " at the words they say.

The tender counsel of an anxious friend,
    The calm reproof in phrase of Holy Writ,
The pleading eyes of one who would amend
    The tangled stitches our weak hands have knit, —
" Songs without words " upon the air they fall,
Words without song we call them, one and all.

It may be that we shall not comprehend
　The subtle chords which so offend us here,
Until we loose our sandals as we wend
　Our way to Paradise, its portals near,
Where many a wandering minstrel wakes to find
That he has left earth's discords far behind.

THE LOVE-TOKEN.

By L. L. Robinson.

A CLOUD had o'er my spirit come, —
　　A cloud that darkened all my light,
And blotting out each star of hope,
　　Enwrapped my soul in rayless night ;
And still it deepened day by day,
Till God Himself seemed far away.

Alone I groped amid the gloom,
　　Alone amid the darkness drear ;
For though I knew that God was true,
　　I could not feel His presence near ;
And human hearts, alas ! are weak,
And yearn to touch the Hand they seek.

" O Thou who hearest prayer," I cried,
　　" Vouchsafe my doubting heart to cheer ;
Some token send, however small,
　　That I may know Thou still art near, —
Some gift so truly Thine alone
That I may know it as Thine own."

In half-unconscious, nameless hope,
　　My trembling hand outstretched to clasp
The mystic gift my yearning heart
　　So vaguely sought and longed to grasp,
And lo ! amid a strange, deep calm,
Some gift seemed laid within my palm.

With heart that almost ceased to beat,
  With trembling joy akin to fear,
I raised my. bowed and drooping head
  To look upon the token dear ;
But — oh, for joy so newly born ! —
Behold my gift, a cruel *thorn !*

With bitter cry my sobbing heart
  Sank crushed, as 'neath a sudden blow.
Was this the answer to my prayer,
  Which only plead His love to know ?
" O God, Thou mightst have spared me scorn !
I asked for love, — behold, a *thorn !* "

But lo ! amid the deepening gloom,
  A low, sweet voice broke on my ear.
" My child," it said, " didst thou not ask
  Some token of My Presence near, —
Some token crave with pleading moan
Which thou shouldst know as Mine alone ?

" Then see ! — from out the chaplet worn
  On my own brow, for love of thee
I 've plucked this one of many thorns,
  Which thou shalt keep for love of Me.
Thou knowest on earth no wealth I own ;
But this, at least, was mine alone."

Could I have dreamt — ah ! could it be ? —
  That in my poor and lonely room
My Saviour thus had really come
  To banish all my doubt and gloom ?
Ah, yes ! The struggling beams of morn
Fell softly on His gift, — my thorn.

And so I keep it hid away,
  Too sacred far for careless eyes,
Deep in my heart, where He alone
  Can see where thus enshrined it lies ;
And when new clouds grow dark and drear,
Its touch assures me *He* is near.

THE LESSON OF THE FLOWERS.

By Flora L. Stanfield.

" I CLAIM the right to be the first to greet Him,"
    Sang the proud rose, her blushing cheek aglow;
" Though every flower that blooms be there to meet Him,
        He would my absence know.
My color tells anew the thrilling story
    Of martyrs going smiling to their death,
My perfume typefies the fragrant glory
        Hid in the censer's breath.
    Oh, let me at His feet my love disclose,
        Because I am a rose."

Then spoke the purple flower of recollection :
    "A pansy is the blossom He would see,
And in the morning of the resurrection,
        His thoughts will turn to me.
My very name will win the priceless treasure
    Of praise from Him who is the world's heart's-ease.
That day you give to Him unstinted measure
        Of love, upon your knees,
Oh, let me, though of beauties I have least,
        Be first to grace His feast."

" I have no boon to crave," said a white lily,
    " Nor any need to claim my rightful place."
Her cheeks were pale, her mien and accents chilly,
        A cloud was on her face.
" What flower should shine in all this fair adorning
    If not the one which mortals name the pure ?
So, on the brightness of the Easter morning,
        My privilege is sure."
Her scorn the heart's-ease stunned ; her hauteur froze
        The ardor of the rose.

O rose, with love in each red petal blooming!
  O pansies, with your faces washed in dew!
O lily, whom to praise would be presuming!
        He needs each one of you!
Love is of earth if purity forsake it,
  And purity is cold if lacking love,
And purest love needs grateful thoughts to make it
        Worthy of place above.
So cease your strife, and all your beauty bring
        To greet the risen King!

PEARLS.

By Callie L. Bonney.

YOU may not see these jewels rare,
    Amid the braids of sunlit hair,
        In beauty gleam;
They deck not hands with queenly grace
Nor add a charm to patient face,
        So like a dream.

With radiant lustre half divine,
Her pearls elsewhere in beauty shine,
        Bright, fair, alway:
One, but the prayer of little child,
Another, life from sin beguiled
        By her sweet way.

The strife and pain her love hath stilled,
The lives her ministry hath filled,
        With blessing fair, —
These are her pearls, that softly glow;
Could any jewel casket show
        Us gems so rare?

AN AUTUMN VOICE.

By Grace C.

THE summer glow has faded from
  The garden, field, and lane:
The blossoms from their sleep of death
  No sun shall wake again.

Not all deserted are the haunts
  Of summer rose and spray:
The autumn blooming lingers yet
  To cheer the short'ning day.

Yet whence the charm of marigold,
  Or china aster gay?
Chrysanthemum or hollyhock,
  The dahlia's bright array?

Or who would seek the golden rod,
  Royal in robe and name,
Yet humblest in its woodland life?
  What magic doth it claim?

The autumn blooming, whence its power?
  What lesson doth it teach?
Sweet summer voices now are mute, —
  Have these no mystic speech?

Less fair and fragrant though they seem,
  These later autumn flowers,
They bear a message, deep as sweet,
  To cheer life's shaded hours.

The spirit which it breathes is hope,
  Triumphant over loss;
Its promise to the victor, life, —
  The crown beyond the cross.

Enduring strength, abiding peace,
　The soul shall gain through gloom ;
Earth's buried hopes immortal rise, —
　Thus speaks the autumn bloom.

Though darker, sadder, grow the days,
　It lingers still to bless,
Its mission one of peace and hope,
　Its might God's tenderness.

THE SHULAMITE.

BY SIDNEY McLEAN.

THE king said to a peasant maid :
　" Come, thou, and be my love.
The best in all my Court so fair —
Apparel rich and jewels rare —
　Are thine, my love, my dove !

" Come, leave thy walks through field and glen !
　Come, leave thy shepherd boy !
Thy face, so full of beauty's force,
Will be a never-ending source
　To me of earthly joy."

" No, no ! " she answered, sadly sweet ;
　" Far rather would I go
With him I love among the lilies, —
To dwell with him among sweet lilies ;
　My heart is where they grow."

The king was much amazed at this, —
　He could not understand
Why from his love she turned aside
To be a simple shepherd's bride,
　And join his lowly band.

But prayers and tears inclined his heart
   To send her on her way, —
With mind so pure and love so meet
To dwell among the lilies sweet,
   In love's most mystic sway.

The prince of this world beckons us
   To come and be his bride.
Oh, listen not !   Thy beacon bright
Is Christ among the lilies white ;
   Thy place is by his side.

LIFE.

By Maria Batterham Lindesey.

HOW beautiful is life when the first dawning
   Touches the sunrise hills,
And all the glint and glow of early morning
   The wide east fills !

How beautiful is life at noontide's hour,
   When, glowing like the sun,
Man's widening pathway, lit with wondrous power,
   Is mapped and run !

How beautiful is life when eventide
   Is stealing softly on,
And sunset's gates are flinging open wide
   Till day is gone !

How beautiful is life when mystic night
   Disrobes her starry breast,
Gleaming with other worlds' far-distant light,
   And man must rest !

Poems of Prayer and Praise.

THE WORLD IS FAIR.

By EMMA SOPHIE STILWELL.

WE will ne'er gie o'er that the warl is fair,
    An' life well worth the livin',
That there 's more o' joy than o' carking care,
    An' o' pleasure than o' grievin'!

The birds sing blithe an' the children play
    In the glad, glad spring together;
An' the trees in the wind hae a merry way
    In the bright or the gruesome weather.

An' hear the trills and throbs o' the brook,
    As it quavers its bass o'er the pebbles,
Or gies out a shower o' silver notes
    In wildring warbling trebles.

Then the liquid idyl of sweet content
    That the pine to the sun rehearses, —
Rare pentameters of orient rhyme,
    Rich incense-breathing verses.

An' the rose with dear, sweet lips o' bloom,
  Blushin' in silent speeches
O' love an' praise to the Maker o' a',
  Such a bonny lesson teaches!

Then we 'll ne'er gie o'er that the warl is fair,
  An' life well worth the livin',
While bird an' bough an' brook an' air
  Are grateful praise outgivin'.

THE GREAT CHANGE.

By the Rev. John May.

BE Thou my light when night prevails,
    My solace in each sore distress,
My Friend when earthly friendship fails,
    My Guide across this wilderness.

As creatures whiten to the snow,
    My soul, reposing at Thy feet,
Shall pure and ever purer grow
    Until the new man is complete.

I would be near Thee if Thou wilt, —
    Be still, and wait, and grow like Thee;
For Thou art goodness — I am guilt,
    But Thou canst take the sin from me.

I want to stay beside Thee, Lord,
    And hold Thy hand, and see Thy face, —
To hear Thy lightest-whispered word,
    To drop the sin, and grasp the grace.

I want the old, the bad, to die;
    I want the new, the good, to grow, —
Till I become another I,
    And Thou alone canst make me so.

I want to do each thing I do
  Before Thy face, Thy smile to see;
To hate the false, to love the true,
  And be what Thou wouldst have me be.

Ah! weak am I. Nor can I keep
  This place beside Thee but a day;
My hands hang feeble and I sleep
  When I would work, or watch, or pray.

O LOVE divine! low at Thy feet
  I prostrate fall.   Hold Thou me fast,
Change, cleanse, re-fashion me complete,
  And fit me for Thy home at last.

CHRISTE, AUDI.

BY THE REV. J. R. NEWELL.

WHEN the morning floods the sky,
    When the noonday sun is high,
When the calm of eve is nigh,
  Hear us, holy Jesu!

When our daily task begins,
And our toil its guerdon wins,
Oh! despite our many sins,
  Hear us, holy Jesu!

While we labor to acquire
That which perisheth, inspire
Something nobler, something higher;
  Hear us, holy Jesu!

And when ends our toil, and we
Mingle in eternity,
May we find ourselves with Thee ;
  Hear us, holy Jesu!

13

THINE THE POWER.

By Frances E Gordon.

FATHER, Thy children own Thy boundless sway
    With common glad accord,
When, asking for our daily bread, we say
    Thine is the power, O Lord!

Thine is the power to give unto Thine own
    All riches earth doth yield,
All perfect gifts that from Thy hand alone,
    Come with sweet promise sealed.

Thine is the power by which we walk the earth
    Cheered by hope's gladdening ray;
The while the happy spirits, Love and Mirth,
    Go with us on our way.

Thine is the gracious power to satisfy,
    If so it be Thy will,
Beyond our utmost thought, each pleading cry,
    Our heart's desire fulfil!

Thine is the power to make Thy soldiers fight
    Victorious over all;
So strong within Thy panoply of light,
    We cannot faint nor fall.

Thy greater power can help us when we meet
    Our foes upon the field,
Wounded and spent, to rise from sore defeat,
    To fall, but not to yield.

Thine, Thine the power to bring us even now
    Where we have longed to be;
Where, with Thy new name written on our brow,
    We shall Thy glory see.

That waking here or there we scarce may know.
    It is Thy kingdom still.

Thine is the power to know our every need, —
    The power to choose and see
Which path of sorrow or of joy will lead
    Thy children nearest Thee.

O Thou, who hast all power in earth and heaven!
    Pour on our souls Thy light;
Help us to take whate'er Thy love has given
    And use Thy gifts aright.

Oh, let us trust Thy boundless power, each day,
    To send us what is best;
To lead us safely by the chosen way
    Unto Thy perfect rest.

LONGING.

ELLA MOONEY.

Out of the depths have I called unto Thee, O Lord. Ps. cxxx.
I will lift up mine eyes unto the hills, from whence cometh my help. Ps. cxxi.

OUT of the depths, unto the hills I call,
        With bowèd face:
" The depths," *my* home, " unto the hills," my All,
        Thy dwelling-place.

What figure could the holy singer use,
　　　More true indeed !
The mount is Thine ; the valley mine, whose dews
　　　My being feed.

O wondrous Sun ! to Thy transcendent height
　　　My spirit take !
Oh, draw me who am parched with thirst Thy might
　　　Alone can slake !

I long to stretch these folded wings; I feel
　　　A life within
Awaiting but Thy-call, to break the seal
　　　Impressed by sin.

As Thou to Lazarus saidst in time of yore,
　　　" Come forth ! " so say
To my imprisoned soul, and she shall soar
　　　To realms of day.

Only a touch, a look of Thine, O King !
　　　Transformeth me
Into a beautiful and holy thing,
　　　And worthy Thee.

Whene'er I pass in worldly courts a day,
　　　With smile for smile;
Joining the chorus of her witching lay
　　　Time to beguile;

At setting sun I am awearied quite,
　　　And ill at ease ;
A lonely heart-sickness steals on with night,
　　　Naught will appease,

Until I humbly turn again to Thee
　　　My Lover true;
Ah! then what comfort, rest, what ecstasy,
　　　Are born anew !

I must be thine.   Naught satisfies, below,
                The craving soul.
Chain the immortal in "the depths?"   Ah, no!
                The *height*, her goal.

And yet, albeit I see in visions rare
                My mountain home,
And hear the spirits of her purer air
                All bid me " come "—

I have no power to climb alone; aid me,
                O Friend Divine!
That I may soar "unto the hills ; " and be
                The glory Thine.

A THANKSGIVING.

By L. P. S.

I AM so blest — I am so blest
        By Thee, my Friend, my King;
My eyes grow dim with thankful tears
        That gather as I sing.

No day but shines Thy sun, within
        A sky of cloudless blue ;
No path but flowers spring up to greet
        Me with their shy — " For you ! "

No eve but brings its soothing peace,
        Though shadows lengthen fast ;
No night but whisper stars to me,
        " There shall be rest at last ! "

Therefore, dear Friend, once crowned with thorns,
        Now crowned with power, my King!
Thou knowest my thanks are true, although
        Tears gather as I sing.

A GRADUAL.[1]

BY THE REV. NELSON AYRES.

PRAISE to Thee, Lord,
  praise be forever given !
Praise on earth ! Praise, too,
  in the highest heaven !
Praise for grace vouchsafed,
  and for sins forgiven,
    Glorious Jesus.

Praise for words, grand,
  sweet, of apostles' writing,
Shining truth-beams, pathway to heaven lighting.
"Other sheep," long lost, to
  the fold inviting,
    Merciful Jesus.

Praise we sing, high praise,
  at the Gospel's reading,
While we see Thee, thou-
  sands with manna feeding,
Thee with blood-mark'd footsteps, to glory leading,
    Suffering Jesus.

[1] In Sapphic strophes.

GRANT US THY PEACE.

By E. M. W.

FAR in the west the day is gently fading,
    Dark fall the shadows of the evening time,
A holy calm all nature is pervading,
    Soft on the ear sings out the vesper chime —
        Grant us Thy Peace.

Lord, since the morn, our erring feet have wandered,
    Far from the way in sorrow and in pain,
With broken vows, and golden moments squandered,
    Weary and sad, we come to Thee again —
        Grant us Thy Peace.

Thou, whose kind heart has throbbed with mortal anguish,
    O'er loved ones gone and sacred trust betrayed,
Thou will not leave our souls in grief to languish ;
    Thou know'st our needs, withhold not then Thine aid —
        Grant us Thy Peace.

Dark grows the night, the weary world is sleeping,
　Yet darkness lurks within its curtained fold ;
May angel bands their loving vigils keeping,
　Grant us, as erst Thy faithful saint of old —
　　Grant us Thy Peace.

Thou, whose dear feet have wandered, torn and bleeding,
　Thro' desert wild, and mountains' rugged way,
We should be lost but for Thy gracious leading ;
　Guide us thro' darkness to the perfect day —
　　Grant us Thy Peace.

A HEART-GARDEN.

By Emma Sophie Stilwell.

CLEANSE this heart, O Lord ! but now
　Roused from wasteful slumber;
Plant the blossoms of Thy grace
　Where but weeds encumber.

Let self-love be banished quite,
　Root out jealous fear,
And let anger's flame be quenched
　By sweet pity's tear.

Thou hast taught that gentleness
　Is the best reproving,
Then let censure yield heart-room
　Unto ruthful loving.

Then will love for humankind
　Spring and bud and flower,
Making sweet to all around
　Morn and evening hour.

LET THEM GIVE THANKS.

By E. S.

IF they give thanks who have known no weeping,
    Have felt no fear, and have wrought no sin,
Their first estate, unfallen, keeping,
    Standing the light of their God within,
Oh, what should *they* give who from weary strife
Have entered the gate of eternal life !

If they give thanks on whose baby faces
    No shame hath passed, whom no sin defiled,
Passing yet pure from love's embraces
    To His arms, who was once a little child.
What thanks should they give whose crimson stain
Is washed in His blood who for them was slain ?

If they give thanks who have served Him ever,
    From childhood's morning through manhood's day,
Their life flowing on like some peaceful river
    That knows no haste, and makes no delay,
What thanks shall they give who have hardly won
Pardon and peace e'er their day is done ?

Let them give thanks whom the Lord, in pity,
    Found in the wilderness, far astray,
And safely led to His holy City,
    With fire by night, and with cloud by day ;
Now, safely within the golden wall,
Let them at His feet adoring fall !

For love that forgave, restored, defended,
    For grace that renewed, sustained, and fed,
For the watchful care that their steps attended,
    For the heavenly hope round their pathway shed,
For the life He gave, and the death He died,
Let them give thanks to the Crucified !

FROM A HAPPY HEART.

By J. C. S.

In all time of our prosperity, Good Lord, deliver us.

NOT with a soul with tempests shaken
     While tossing on life's, troubled sea,
Not with a heart oppressed, forsaken,
     Come I, O gracious Lord, to Thee, —
No load of care, no hidden grief,
Moves me to seek Thy kind relief.

Nay, 't is the mercies that surround me, —
     The sunbeams bright, the blossoms fair,
These loving hearts I see around me,
     This wish fulfilled, that answered prayer,
Bright memories, and hopes more sweet, —
These bring me to Thy sacred feet.

I ask not now for strength in sorrow,
     Or comfort for an aching heart,
In fear lest thou should'st bid to-morrow
     These blessings suddenly depart;
Ah, no! — the grace for which I pray
Is to bear joy aright to-day;

To take each separate gift or pleasure
     As token of that tender care
Which I can never fully measure,
     Yet know surrounds me everywhere,
And, though my sunshine turn to night,
Still guides my wavering steps aright.

O Father, let no bliss thou sendest,
     Fill utterly this wayward heart;
And while I take the joy Thou lendest
     Make me content therewith to part,
When Thou shalt bid me yield to Thee
E'en that which choicest seems to me;

And keep before my spirit ever
  The sense of my unworthiness,
For what I am, whom thou dost never
  Forget to comfort and to bless!
Yes, let me always humbled be
By each bright gift Thou sendest me.

"WE WOULD SEE JESUS."

By the Rev. J. Anketell.

" WE would see Jesus!" Dark the shadows gather,
  The lingering light of day is almost done;
We raise our weeping eyes to Thee, O Father,
  And pray Thee: Manifest to us Thy Son!

"We would see Jesus!" Angry shouts defy Him,
  Proud science curls the lip at One it scorns;
Blind Pharisee and Sadducee deny Him,
  Wearing another cruel crown of thorns.

"We would see Jesus!" Now His face is hidden,
  The clouds receive Him up to realms of light;
Yet in the Sacrament His Love has bidden,
  He stands revealed by faith to mortal sight.

"We would see Jesus!" Haste the happy morning,
  That gives bright sunlight to a soul redeemed.
Long have we watched through darkness for its dawning;
  Oh, long and dreary has our vigil seemed!

"We would see Jesus!" Mocked and in derision
  Our eyes have seen Thee, scourged and crucified;
Hasten, O Lord, the Beatific Vision,
  That sees Thee seated at Thy Father's side!

WORK AND PRAYER.

BY L. D. S.

FIRST VOICE.

NOW shineth the rising sun into thy bower;
    Work! Day calleth loudly on thee for thy task;
Thy brain with its thought, thine arm with its power,
    Await but to do what thy spirit shall ask;
Fuse thought, power, and love in the work of the hour.

SECOND VOICE.

Ah! brighter is God than the sun in his might.
    Pray! Souls are not living that breathe not in prayer.
Thy life is a vapor, swift passing from sight.
    The soul never dieth; let *that* be thy care,
Lest, affrighted, thou hear thy Lord's voice at the night.

FIRST VOICE.

Time spent on the knees is time lost in the race.
    Work! He loves not the idler; and bread must be got.
Thy children's low cry, the tears on the face
    Of the wife who bemoaneth thy labor forgot —
Art thou deaf? Art thou blind? Seeking phantom-like
      grace?

SECOND VOICE.

Harsher sound in thine ear will the dread wailing be
    Of children thrust out from the kingdom of heaven.
They who wait on the Lord e'er they perish shall see
    The ravens bring food, rocks by water-springs riven.
Love for children and wife! Did not Christ *die* for thee?

THIRD VOICE.

Peace, ye wranglers! Why part ye what God hath made
    one?
    For He that gave prayer is the same that gave toil;
Therefore pray from the morn till the light is no more;
    Yet no moment from work let thy tired hand recoil
Till the task that was given at even is o'er.

Prayer is work; and no work without prayer shall be
    blest.
Work is prayer, if for Jesus our Saviour 't is done.
Nerve thine arm with thy prayer, let thy work fire thy
    breast,
And when into thy bower slants the slow setting sun
Thy soul and thy body shall find each its rest.

MEDITATION

Poems of Meditation.

GRASPING AT SHADOWS.

By Irene Griswold.

SUCH a beautiful spray !
   Just before me it lay
On the walk that was flooded with light,
   One would scarcely believe
   That the touch could deceive,
So real it was to the sight.

   Yet, on stooping to grasp,
   It eluded my clasp,
Though the form was so clearly defined
   That I certainly knew
   From the shadow in view
The substance was somewhere behind.

   Through the light of God's love
   The things from above
Cast beautiful shadows below.
   These shadows I see, —
   They prove clearly to me
The substance is somewhere, I know.

WASTED.

By Flora L. Stanfield.

DEAR little hour! if I could call you back,
    I would not chase a vagrant butterfly
And let your blessings slip so idly by.
Oh, come again adown the year's swift track!
No care of mine shall your sweet moments lack
        If you will but come back!

Calm little day! why did you fade so soon?
    A day is long, I thought, and so I dreamed
    Away the golden hours; it only seemed
A moment till the bells rang in the noon;
A moment more, and God hung out the moon.
        Why did you fade so soon?

Glad little year! where has your brightness fled?
    I prized you; but I said, " So many days
    Make up the year that I will tread the ways
The world has marked."   But when with heart that bled
I sought my little year — my year was dead!
        Where had its brightness fled?

So now I hasten up and down the street,
    And call to each and all, " Oh! can you say
    If any year of mine has strayed this way?
Or if a wandering day or hour you meet,
I pray you tell me, and I 'll run to greet
        Its joys with flying feet."

And thus I look for hour and day and year
    That I have missed so long; perchance to some
    Unlooked-for place each waiting one will come
To greet me; so I will be patient here,
And pray that your lost glory may be near,
        Dear hour, calm day, glad year!

THE ORGANIST.

BY EDWARD HENRY ECKEL.

HE sits him down at twilight hour
  Before the ivory keys,
And lets his fingers wander o'er
  The clavier as they please.

The dreamer plays, and lets his dreams
  Take form whate'er they will, —
Sometimes in diapasons full,
  Or voices small and shrill.

And as he sits with whitened locks,
  Unbinding harmonies
That speechless lie in soundless chains
  Beneath the placid keys,

A golden ray from blazoned pane
  Streams in through pictured saint,
And bending o'er him musing there,
  Creates a picture quaint.

Transfigured in the waning light,
  A youth once more he seems ;
Each silvery lock, no longer white,
  With golden sunlight gleams.

The decades passed since youth was his
  Like broken dreams appear ;
And like a dream this Evensong
  To weary souls so dear.

The choristers have sung their psalms,
  And priest the lessons read ;
But still absorbed the dreamer plays,
  To other fancies dead.

14

The pictured glass is dark again;
　The flowing locks are white .
The organ, moaning, dies in pain,
　As dies the fading light.

Though dark and still the empty church.
　An angel flies o'erhead,
And passing near with drooping wings,
　He leaves the dreamer — dead.

REVERIE.

By Castelmar.

WHITE little sails far cut at sea,
　　I watch ye, painted athwart the blue.
The clouds a-dream in the sky above,
　And ye at rest on the same soft hue.

October is rocking the earth to sleep, —
　With dreamy zephyrs is crooning low ;
Full soon the November winds will heap
　Above its slumbers the sheltering snow.

How strange to think that all this glow
　And glad abundance of life will lie
So many brooding months benumbed, —
　Breathless and dumb, 'neath a leaden sky !

O clouds and sails and earth at rest,
　Have ye not a lesson to teach my heart,
As it feels its winter chill come on
　And the battling winds and storms upstart ?

Oh, that it too might learn to rest
　Safe in the shelter our God doth mark,
Close and still on the Father's breast,
　Shuddering not at the storm and dark !

I wonder are they afraid — the flowers ?
  Do they tire of waiting, and long to grow ?
Do roses weep through the winter hours,
  And violets shiver beneath the snow ?

I fear me much 't is my heart alone
  That questions the Hand outstretched to lead,
And makes its weak, repining moan, —
  " Dost Thou forget my piteous need ? "

Poor heart, sore heart, God pity thee,
  And clasp thee close and hold thee fast !
God pardon thine infirmity,
  And bring thy summer back at last !

"O VANISHED DAY !"

By F. BURGE GRISWOLD.

THE night is come, O vanished day !
    What record hast thou borne away ?
The early dawn was fair and bright,
With wishes pure, and purpose right.

What of the hours ?   Have Faith and Love
Been diligent themselves to prove
My guardian angels, covering
Both speech and act with shining wing ?

Has Truth been near me with her brow
As sunlight on the driven snow ?
And Joy and Peace — have these stayed by,
With an unwearied constancy ?

What graces have I entertained ?
What sinful inclinations chained ?
Have heart and hands been freely given
In holy charities, to Heaven ?

Was every passing moment fraught
With good, in word, or deed, or thought?
The night is come, O vanished day!
What record hast thou borne away?

UNDER THE TREES.

By Julia E Phelps.

AS friends, dear life-long friends, we love the trees;
High o'er our heads they rise, a lordly race,
Yet spread their leafy tents with genial grace,
And ever tireless stand to serve and please.

The same to-day as when our lives began;
Beside the cottage door or palace gate,
In majesty and constancy they wait,
While come and go the brief, swift days of man.

The timid bird that from the gentlest hand
A crumb will scarcely take, casts out all fear
Amid their leafy boughs, and sweet and clear
Trills out its joyous lays o'er all the land.

The homeless wanderer, whose clouded mind,
Perchance, tho' rough the way his feet have trod,
Still holds some lingering ray of trust in God,
Their cool shade seeks, a touch of peace to find.

Upon those distant scenes that vanish not,
Where memory loves to wander down the past,
Unchanged the trees their peaceful shadows cast,
The leaflet's silvery tones are unforgot.

Here, resting, dreaming, listening, free from care,
New visions reach this poor, dim, mortal sight,
The mist uplifts that hid the heavenly light,
The soul communes with God in silent prayer.

"AS WE LOOK UPON THE DEAD."

BY ROSE HARTWICK THORPE.

STANDING by the open coffin,
 Where the icy hand of death,
Sweeping over cheek and forehead,
 Chilled the face and hushed the breath,
We forget each hasty action,
 All the angry words they said;
We remember only goodness
 When we look upon the dead!

And we sometimes think so sadly:
 "Could those closed eyes see again,
Could that still heart only quicken
 With a throb of joy or pain,
We would shield them from all evil."
 But, alas! the day has fled;
And our tears lie all unheeded,
 On the still face of the dead.

Do we ever think, I wonder,
 That some struggling heart might be
Strengthened in the path of duty
 By a smile from you or me, —
Some despairing one grow hopeful
 Could these tears for them be shed,
If we only gave the living
 Half the love we give the dead?

Oh! the erring need our pity:
 Haply, could the truth be known,
They will bear a clearer record
 To the Father than our own.
All these tears are unavailing,
 Though in deepest sorrow shed,
When we keep them from the living
 Just to give them to the dead.

IN MAY.

By O. W. ROGERS.

FROM books, and care, and vagrant thought,
    I go to Nature's fair domain,
To see the wonders Spring hath brought
    From peaceful death to life again.

The grass up-springs with grateful dower
    And lines my pathway to the wood,
Where mosses feel th' enlivening power
    Nor languish in humilitude.

The wind-flower nods from hazel-hedge,
    The violet coy peers up at me ;
And columbine, on yonder ledge,
    Gives a "good morrow ! " fair and free.

Ferns, velvet-clad, awake and bring
    Their grace to shade the limpid pool,
Whence tiny rills o'erflow and sing
    A welcome sweet in cadence cool.

How fairy-like the woodland scene !
    Each tree apparelled daintily,
Seems conscious of its charms, I ween,
    And buds and leaves impatiently.

The maple blushes in its blooms,
    Forecasting its October sheen ;
The birch shakes out her tasselled plumes
    And rightful reigns the forest queen.

How lush the meadow-grasses grow,
    And spread rich feast for meek-eyed kine !
The becks how joyously they flow
    And glisten in the soft sunshine !

The cowslip opes its golden cup
  And mocks the sun this glorious day;
All earth seems mounting up and up,
  And heaven seems meeting her half-way !

O Nature's peace ! O Nature's balm !
  My God, I thank Thee more and more
For her sweet influence — holy, calm —
  And for her beauty's boundless store !

I thank Thee for a friend at one
  With me, in love of field and wood,
Who sees in mountain, mead, or stone,
  A token of Thy love and good.

Though girt with man's infirmities,
  He looks through Nature unto Thee,
And leaves the world's inanities
  To go a-field with Thee and me !

THE CHANGING LEAF.

By J. W. P.

THE forest trees are all aglow
  With ruby hues aflame ;
Topaz and garnet high and low,
And tinctures rare, each nook doth show,
  Which artist scarce can name.

On Nature's pallet she hath spread
  Her pigments mixed with care ;
And o'er the woodland wastes are shed
The radiant flora of her bed,
  With glories everywhere !

She takes what hues she liketh best
  To trace her story in ;
Snatching her tints from rosy west,
Or borrowing from the jewelled crest
  Where morning doth begin.

And when the gallery is full
  Of visions none can paint ;
With frosted brush, these works of skill,
Are from the canvas swept at will,
  In wealth of lavishment !

And so with each returning year
  The picture is renewed :
The Master-artist doth appear,
To garnish thus the grateful cheer
  Of autumn's bounteous good !

MAY.

By Cornelia Bogert.

THE May has come.   The earthworms go
  To sun themselves above the ground :
Birds warble on the trees around,
And brooks respond in rhythmic flow.

We feel oppressed by sudden heat,
  The tender ferns are involute.
  The fruit-trees promise give of fruit,
May-flowers spring up at our feet

What though the idle frogs may croak,
  Our hearts are like the brooks, set free,
  That pour their fulness in the sea ;
Unheeding discontented folk.

Baptized in showers through the night,
  The clovers sweet their censers swing;
  Bird-choristers are carolling;
The apple-trees are veiled in white.

The willow, ironwood, and birch
  Put forth their leaves, the violets blow,
  As down the winding road we go,
And quiet, enter in the church.

We feel, while we are kneeling there,
  Our Confirmation vows to take,
  As though the works of God would make
The words more earnest in our prayer.

As if His Spirit, like a dove,
  With peace which passeth what we know,
  Would make us consecrated grow,
To turn our thoughts to Him above.

THE RECLUSE.

By O. W. Rogers.

FAR from September's wealth of blooms,
  On mountain, moor, and lea,
Like one who fearlessly assumes
  The privilege to be,

A solitary aster stands
  Where flows Weelahka's stream
By rugged rocks and woody strands,
  Ere lapsing into dream.

Oh, not from mossy sod it rears,
  Its lissom stalk and straight,
But from a rock where passing years
  Have left a lichened state.

An exile is it from the moor,
  Or from the bosky wood,
Like one who on some siren's shore
  Ponders in mystic mood?

It seems to watch the waters pass
  On, on eternally,
Like some charmed sentry whom, alas!
  No comrade shall set free.

A hermit is it, or a monk,
  In this so sweet retreat,
Passing, in meditation sunk,
  An *Ave!* to repeat?

A nun, from blest community
  Of sisters on yon hill,
Wrapt in rare opportunity
  To gaze and dream at will?

It is, I trow, a flower of grace
  Keeping its vigil lone,
Above the water's reckless race
  By its huge bowlder stone.

Nodding in every breath of wind,
  Gleaming in sunny sheen,
Its welcome is a welcome kind,
  Its lesson clearly seen.

Fair queen, I love thy wild domain,
  Yet wonder when I see
The peaceful tenure of thy reign
  On yon sterility.

Oh, may my heart interpret free,
  When on thy realm I muse.
The sweet content I learn of thee,
  Thou beautiful recluse!

CARMINA IN NOCTE.

By the Rev. J. Anketell.

WITH sorrow weeping, my lone watch keeping
　　While all are sleeping, —
　　　The stars my light, —
Though fond hopes perish, His love I cherish,
　　Who giveth songs in the silent night.

I muse and ponder, my thoughts still wander
And seek Him yonder
　　In glory bright,
Forever living, my sin forgiving,
　　Who giveth songs in the silent night.

Then upward soaring, my love adoring
Its song is pouring,
　　With sweet delight,
Where saints are praising His love amazing,
　　Who giveth songs in the silent night.

With accents tender, their praise they render
In white-robed splendor
　　On Syon's height,
To One victorious, forever glorious,
　　Who giveth songs in the silent night.

Break, Day of glory, and tell the story
Of ages hoary,
　　And Time's long flight;
Though earth should perish, His love I cherish,
　　Who giveth songs in the silent night.

UNDER MAGDALEN TOWER: A MAY MEMORY.[1]

BY KATHARINE A. MATHEW.

THE springtime sunshine's gentle balm
  Falls softened in a golden haze,
And sloping lawns of tender green
  Spread out beside the trodden ways.
The breath and light of budding May
  Steep lawn and glade in beauty rare;
And round, white clouds drift on their way
  Through the soft azure of the air.

A wind swept down the western hills
  And tossed the opening lilac blooms;
It swayed the nodding Guelder-rose,
  And waved the bright laburnum plumes.
The stately chestnut's spreading shade
  Was lit with white lamps tipped with flame;
In leafy alleys breezes made
  A murmurous sound that went and came, —

That went and came, and rose and fell,
  And brought upon its fragrant wings
The echo of the Matin-bell
  That in the old tower hangs and swings,
And flings its iron music out,
  Bidding good souls to chant and pray
And lift the heart to the dear God,
  Who sends the sunshine and the May.

And while the echoes faintly die
  The cloistered stillness wakes again
To young boy-voices, clear and high,
  That chant a metrical refrain;

[1] By the will of Henry the Seventh, of England, it was ordained that a Mass for the repose of his soul should be sung at five o'clock on the morning of the first of May, on the summit of Magdalen Tower, Oxford, "forever." A service including the *Hymnus Eucharisticus* is now yearly sung at that time and place.

And up the winding tower-stairs
   Climbs (two by two, I see them go)
A troop of white-robed choristers,
   With fresh young faces all a-glow.

I catch the beaming of bright eyes
   That veil as best they can their mirth
(For hearts are light when life is May,
   And a boy's gladness is of earth).
They pass ; the chant, the mounting feet
   Die into silence ; I, alone
Beneath the old tree's rustling shade,
   Catch now and then a falling tone.

The cool, clear Cherwell's quiet deeps
   Reflect the elm-trees overhead.
My thoughts sail down the long, long ways
   To old May-days and springs long fled,
When the stern king, whose grief-worn heart,
   Bereft of peace, craved earnest prayer
From Christian souls, who tenderly
   Would lift a solemn worship there.

So the sweet music mounts, aspires,
   And echoes through the crystal air ;
And holy Eucharistic hymn
   Floats heavenward with the chanted prayer :
The whole wide earth seems kneeling low,
   Lifting her suppliant hands to Him
Whose glory fills the universe,
   Midst echoing songs of cherubim.

A requiem song earth's children raise
   At eve or morn, — " Lord, give us peace ! "
Give us, in mercy. quiet days :
   Let strife be hushed ; let warfare cease.
" The peace of God," — sweet, parting words
   That close the prayer and speed us on !
O'er heart and mind they softly fall
   Till strife be past and victory won.

MONTREUX.

BY THE REV. FRANK L. NORTON.

A S one who, dreaming in the twilight gloom,
   Sees loved and lost ones, indistinct and dim,
Friends of his younger days, who go and come
   With pleasant memories, — not spectres grim
And ugly phantasies, but with that mien
   They wore in time when hope was young and bright,
When faith was theirs in things not plainly seen,
   And day was theirs, nor yet had come the night,
So, fair Montreux, within thy sheltered nooks
   I sit and dream; while that dear form and face
Which, in my boyhood's days, with eager looks,
   Made holiday in this enchanted place,
Comes back again, — my sainted father's soul, —
   And holds communion sweet with me.
As then the moonlight quivers on the vine-clad knoll;
   As then the lake round Chillon's towers I see.
I hear him speak of what the mountains teach:
   " They bring my soul," he says, " a holy calm, —
A *peace* beyond the power of Care to reach, —
   And bathe my tirèd soul with restful balm.

When on the eternal hills my eyes have rest,
  So strong and brave, unmoved by stormy blast,
To them, like wearied dove unto her nest,
  Myself would flee and find a home at last.
Their path to Heaven is rough and hard to gain ;
  Their way is steep and often lost in cloud ;
But when the heights are reached by might and main,
    White robes are given with which their forms they
      shroud ;
And round their heads, with ever growing light,
    Th' eternal Sun shines forth with welcoming ray,
The while their earth-bound feet in dreary night
  Are stumbling in the darkness of the way.
God's altars they within His temple spread
  With the ' fair linen ' of the virgin snow ;
The ripening wheat provides the Living Bread,
  And vineyards redden with Eucharistic glow ;
While rose-hued mists, like incense-laden air,
  Rise at the vesper hour in clouds as bright
As in cathedral choir ascending prayer
  Is wafted upward toward the realms of light.
God make our inmost thought as clear and white
  As the fair vestments of these altars be, —
Purged, like the Rhone, emerging pure and bright
  From Leman's font to join the deep blue sea ! "

"I STAND AT THE DOOR, AND KNOCK."

BY F. MACRAE.

" HE called me to Him in my early morn,
      When, full of glee,
  I played and sang upon the grassy lawn
      Beneath the tree ;
  But like a wayward colt I turned again
  Back to my games in scorn, — I came not then.

"Again He called me on a later day
    When years were gone, —
When I had ceased to laugh and sing and play
    Beneath the sun,
When like 'a stricken deer I left the herd:'
But oh! I came not at that pleading word.

"Once more He called me at the evening time
    Of my poor life, —
He stopped and called me when my eyes were dim
    With age and strife:
Oh! then at last I came, and found my rest
Within the shelter of my dear Lord's breast.

"Yet ever does this thought disturb my dreams
    By night and day,
Whether in busy throngs or by the woodland streams
    I take my way:
Oh, would that I had come long years before! —
When first I heard that kind knock at my door."

"TELL ME A TALE."

By Fannie A. D. Darden.

TELL me a beauteous tale;
    Tell me the story that I love the best, —
You know it, mother, — sweeter than the rest;
'T is not a tale of fairies on the wing,
Nor huntsmen wild that make the forest ring,
Nor fancied image of uncanny thing, —
    Tell me a truthful tale!

    Tell me the tale I love, —
The same old story you so oft have told,
Brighter than gems, and richer far than gold, —

15

Of Bethlehem's Babe to whom the wise men came,
Whom shepherds worshipped by that holy name
Of Christ the Lord : I feel my heart aflame
    At that sweet tale of love !

Tell me a wondrous tale ;
Tell me some ardent, glowing tale of truth
To lead my spirit upward ! cried the youth.
They tell me life is thorny, rough, and drear :
Tell me the story of the Saviour dear,
Who with true strength and help is ever near :
    Tell me the wondrous tale !

Tell us the blessed tale,
O preacher to the longing souls of men !
Tell us the oft-told story o'er again.
You need no honeyed praise to gild the word
Which pierces hearts as with a two-edged sword ;
The Spirit to thy speech will aid afford :
    Tell us the blessed tale !

Tell us the old, old tale
Of Jesus dying for the sins of men ;
Tell it in simple words, and oft again,
To rich and poor, the ignorant and the wise, —
It needs no words in rhetoric's florid guise
To teach the heart or ope the blinded eyes :
    Tell us the oft-told tale !

Tell me the precious tale,
The old man said upon his dying bed ;
Tell me of Him who for my soul hath bled,
Who on the cross gained victory o'er the grave,
My Saviour Christ, whose hand is strong to save, —
Blest story chanted over Jordan's wave,
    The immortal, deathless tale !

MY PORTION FOREVER.

BY M. E. BEAUCHAMP.

I CANNOT live without Thee,
   O Jesus, Friend Divine;
I long to feel Thy Presence
   Within this heart of mine.
Thou nearest and Thou dearest Friend,
   Without Thee earth were gloom,
And life were but the dreary way
   To an unlighted tomb.

I cannot live without Thee;
   No earthly joy or love
Can fill the heart that yearneth
   For Thee, all things above.
In Thee alone my heart exults,
   My Love, my Joy, my All;
While Thou art mine no bliss can blind,
   No terrors can appall.

I cannot live without Thee,
   O Shepherd of my soul,
To guide me and to guard me
   And all my ways control;
Poor, homeless wanderer I should be
   Without the unseen Guide
By whom my path in life is marked,
   My every want supplied.

I cannot live without Thee;
   Thou art my breath of life,
My strength in every hardship,
   My aid in every strife.
Uncheered by Thee, life's loneliness
   Would be too hard to bear;
And heaven would be no heaven to me
   If Thou should'st not be there.

Poems of Childhood.

---◆---

DAISY'S EASTER GIFT.

By Callie L. Bonney.

DAISY sat in the family pew,
  As sweet as the Easter blossoms fair,
A wond'ring look in the violet eyes,
  The sunshine lighting her golden hair.

Listening intently to chant and creed,
  In tiny prayer-book keeping the place,
Reading softly with smile of content,
  An eager look on the dimpled face.

When, 'mid the service of prayer and song —
  Could it be? — a purring soft and low!
And out of the depths of Daisy's muff,
  Walked bright-eyed kitten as white as snow.

And when they questioned her afterward,
  The wee one answered, in accents glad,
" You said we should bring an Easter gift,
  And that was the bestest thing I had."

LINES ON THE PICTURE OF A CHILD.

BY O. W. ROGERS.

DEAR child, with eyes of truth untold,
　With lightsome face and hair of gold,
Thy picture, 'mid my books, out-gleams
Like happy thought from sombre dreams.

Spring sunlight on thy lips appears,
Presaging neither doubt nor fears;
Hope dwelleth there, and in thine eyes
A beauty that with April vies.

Like modest violet in the wood,
Uprearing in sweet solitude,
So pure, so guileless, and bedight
With subtle influence of delight.

Sweet child, thy bright, unclouded face
Looks on me with a peerless grace,
And in this darkling winter day
Diffuses all the sheen of May.

Like crystal lens through it I see
Thy sponsor's love and fealty —
See through thine own her trustful eyes,
And trace her path to Paradise.

O Linda, may her grace be thine,
Her prayers thy daily needs entwine;
A woman's heart, a woman's will
God give thee, shielded by His skill!

Oh, with thy years may graces shine,
O'ershadowed by a grace Divine!
Then what is now so fair to see
Shall fairer than the promise be!

PATTY GRIMM.

BY CLARA J. DENTON.

PRAY, have you heard of Patty Grimm?
  A most unfortunate child is she:
When you have heard her story through.
  I 'm sure you 'll quite agree with me.

For Patty's eyes can only see
  The faults and flaws in everything;
She whines o'er this, and frets at that,
  Till peace and happiness take wing.

Alas! poor child, what can she do?
  There 's nothing right in life below.
The sky 's too blue, or else too dark.
  And time too fast, or else too slow.

A book 's too dull, or else too light,
  Her friends too gay, or stupid all.
Her work too hard, her play too rough.
  Her clothes too large, or else too small.

From day to day she plucks life's thorns
  And throws the flowers fair away,
Alas! alas! she must become
  A very thorny Miss, some day!

Her face has quite forgotten all
  The tender smiles of baby days:
Her frowns — alack! so fast they come
  Her brow is like a woody maze.

What can we do for Patty Grimm?
  For this is what we sorely dread,
That, should she reach sweet Heaven at last.
  She 'll wish 't was somewhere else instead.

TWO BIRTHDAYS.

By M. E. BEAUCHAMP.

A FAIR–HAIRED little maiden
    Looks up with beaming eyes;
She tells me 't is her birthday,
    With a kind of mild surprise ;
So odd it seems to her small brain,
    She cannot well divine
Why she was eight but yesterday,
    And now, to-day, is nine.

Her mind is full of projects
    About her sports and toys ;
No fear of coming evil
    Her present good alloys ;
She only wants the tender care,
    Her parents freely give,
And in the shelter of their love,
    Without a care can live.

  .   .   .   .   .

A sad-eyed, gray-haired woman
    Sits in her room alone :
It is her birthday morning,
    And memory makes a moan,
That three-score years have passed away,
    And taken in their train
All hopes and joys, and left to her
    But weariness and pain.

Ah ! lonely one, bethink thee
    Of that far birthday morn,
When life seemed full of brightness,
    Thy path without a thorn.
If thou again could'st freely trust
    Thy Father to provide,
Still might'st thou, like little child,
    Without a care abide.

A LITTLE CHILD.

BY MRS. J. D. H. BROWNE.

A TENDER bud in which enfolded lies
   Life's unexpanded flower —
An opening dawn of endless destinies,
   A heaven-descended dower.

Grasping love's sceptre in a tiny hand,
   All in unconscious state,
It lies and rules, with absolute command,
   A new-born potentate !

Poor mortals, wearing on our tired brow
   The earthly travel-stain,
We see this babe, pure as the driven snow,
   With joy akin to pain.

We see our manhood and our womanhood,
   Veiled in this sweet disguise,
Our own lost possibilities of good
   In these pure, wondering eyes.

Ah ! little pilgrim, better be thy road,
   With less of thorns and snares,
Than that we travelled ! lighter be thy load,
   And fewer be thy cares !

Yet cannot all our tender love avert
   Life's errors and its pains :
We cannot gather out the stones that hurt,
   Nor wash away the stains !

Hadst Thou not said, of old, in Galilee —
   Outstretching hands Divine,
"Suffer the little ones to come to me,"
   And, blessing, made them Thine :

Did we not know Thee as the Guide and Friend,
　Could we not trust to Thee,
To lead these little feet e'en to the end,
　More tenderly than we,

Well might we fear fierce sun and chilling wind,
　And roughness of the way!
But Thou, O Shepherd, ever strong and kind,
　Wilt be Thy lamb's sure stay.

CHILD WISDOM.

By J. C. S.

"O MOTHER, wipe my tears away!"
　　I heard a little maiden say,
Although her mother's stern surprise
Had brought the tears to those sweet eyes.

Dear little one! full well she knew
Though mother chides, she comforts too:
One moment she must needs reprove,
But naught can change her tender love.

Children of larger growth are we,
But oft this truth we fail to see,
That He alone can balm bestow
Who caused the bitter tears to flow.

Though His rebuke has made us mourn,
Our penitence He will not scorn,
If, like the little child, we say,
"Dear Father, wipe our tears away!"

THE CHILDREN.

By Marion Couthouy Smith.

THEY take my very heart — I know not how —
 So shyly lifting up their deep, sweet eyes,
 Pure as the morning star in virgin skies,
'Neath the soft hair and white, unshadowed brow.

I would not that the darkness of the world
 Should cloud their tender light! I would instead
 That mine own eyes should weep, and o'er my head
The wings of storm and sorrow be unfurled.

I fain would stand before each little breast,
 A loving shield ; but since this may not be,
 I long instead that they should turn to me,
As birds that flutter gladly to the nest,
After the first weak flight, sure, ever sure,
To find a mother-heart, and rest secure !

THE HIGHER WISDOM.

By Frederick H. Kelsey.

"O PAPA!" cried little Daisy,
 With a sadness in her eye,
As she saw the kernels scattered,
 'Neath the heavy soil to die.

"O Papa!" cried little Daisy,
 "Do not throw the wheat away :
It must be wrong to waste it,
 It is good for food, you say."

Did the father cease from sowing?
  No; he kissed her tears away;
Bade her wait until the autumn,
  Showed her then the harvest gray.

Thus do we, like little children,
  Raise our foolish human cries,
When the wisdom of our Father
  Some fond hope our heart denies.

But in God's eternal harvest
  We shall find that richest joys
Have been won by our surrender
  Of these pleasing, earthly toys.

So we pray in trustful accents,
  As we journey day by day,
That His will may be accomplished
  And His wisdom point the way.

"GIVE US THIS DAY OUR DAILY BREAD.'

BY THE REV. FRANK L. NORTON, D. D.

LITTLE white-robed, curly head,
  Kneeling down by snowy bed,
Nightly prayers had softly said,
Asking for his " daily bread,"
While he prayed, " Thy will be done
By all dwellers 'neath the sun,
As by those in Heaven above,
Bound to each with bands of love."
Thinking then, with knitted brow,
Of some puzzling " why or how,"
Turning to me, gravely said:
" Papa, tell me, why for bread

Should I ask at even prayer,
Or for food have any care,
When I lay me down to sleep
Asking God my soul to keep?
For I say, 'Give us this day'
When 't is night I kneel to pray.
Seems to me, I 'd better ask
Help to do the morrow's task
Than to pray for bread to eat
'Ere another sun we greet."
Smiled I at the puzzled brow,
Thinking of this " why and how; "
Gently stroked the sunny hair
With its golden color rare,
Shading dreamy, thoughtful eyes,
Catching shadows from the skies.
" Little white-robed, curly head,
When you ask for daily bread,
'T is no selfish prayer you say,
And 't is always somewhere day.
When you pray, 'Give us this day'
Daily bread, you mean to pray
'Give Thy children, everywhere,
Food in answer to my prayer.'
When you lay you down to sleep
Asking God your soul to keep,
It is day in heathen lands —
China's shores and Afric's sands
So you ask for God to give
Heathen children bread to live, —
Bread that cometh down from Heaven,
Food that Christ Himself hath given.
Day by day you ask this food,
Heavenly manna, pure and good.
Give to us this daily bread,
Morn and eve, let it be said;
For 't is always somewhere day,
And you therefore humbly pray
For God's children everywhere,
When you say your evening prayer."

Miscellaneous Poems.

— ◆ —

"AS WHITE AS WOOL."

By Alice Gray Cowan.

"AS white as wool!" Oh, thus, my Saviour said.
    "Thy sins shall be, that now as scarlet are."
My Heavenly Father's word! I bow my head;
    What can I hope for, more? What promise rare?
Behold the flocks upon the far hill-side,
    Like knots of daisies in the tender grass.
Through the dark vales they wander without guide:
    'Neath starry skies the summer nights they pass.
"As white as wool!" — as pure as helpless lambs
    That gambol on the meadow's daisied breast;
That follow, bleating, by the mother's side,
    Or lie upon the streamlet's brink to rest.
My sins, though scarlet, "white as wool" shall be,
    If I but live, my Father, near to Thee!

A SPRING-DAY HYMN.

By the Rt. Rev. W. E. McLaren, D. D., D. C. L.

HOW pure the dawn, and bright!
    A thousand songs of waking joy arise;
And to the zenith, flooding all the skies,
    Mounts the wide splendor of the light.
      So rise, my soul, to God.

Filled are the curving brooks
With hastening streams and waters running bright,
Dancing and singing in the morning light,
    Or gliding into grassy nooks.
      So flow, my life, toward God.

I look for flowers to bloom
Along the margin of these streams; the skies
Of warmer May, with many a fond surprise
    Of violets, shall cheer my gloom.
      Thus do I hope in God.

All Nature turns her face
Toward the increasing sun, and prays the fire
That kindles life and bids the buds conspire
    To clothe the earth with forms of grace.
      Thus I aspire to God.

The day wanes to its close.
The drowsy herd turns homeward, and the wing
Of every bird is folded; vespers ring,
    And weary hearts seek soft repose.
      So rest, my heart! in God.

A SONNET.

By N. F.

I BROKE my lute, and said that I no more
   Would sing, — hopes wrecked, joys past, and
     present pain,
And life not worth the living; all was vain,
   But to sit still and wait upon the shore,
   Whence every moment sadly launches o'er
The vast, unfathomable, trackless main,
And never back returns, the ghostly train
   Of those I love, and shall for aye deplore.
My food was bitter, and the world a jest;
And yet anon a voice spake in my ear ;
   " O son of man " — and broke my slothful rest —
   " O son of man," it said, " what dost thou here ?
To labor, though no fruit appear, were best,
   Nor idle to be found when, lo ! thy judge is near.'

BY THE SEA.

By the Rev. J. H. Knowles.

FAR off, the rocks point out to sea,
   With steadfast, true, unswerving hand;
The winds may blow, the waves may dash,
   But ever constant, there they stand.
A symbol this, O God, that we
Should ever fix our thoughts on Thee.

They stand 'mid tumult of the storm,
   They stand when lisping waves caress ;
In sunshine, rain-mist, or deep shade,
   They show no sign of weariness.
A symbol this, of trustful rest,
That what God sends is always best.

HEROISM ON THE SEA.

By Maria Batterham Lindsey.

IT was to the shore of a boisterous sea,
Tossing and heaving in terrible glee,
Through the rough waves' lash and the wild winds' play
That a brave ship drove one winter's day.

She struck on the shoal of St. George's strand,
In sight and almost within hail of land,
And the waves washed over the vessel's side,
When an anchored boat her distress descried.

The ship was fast, and the sea ran high,
And the cruel wind went screaming by, —
It tore her shrouds and tattered her sail,
As she bent to her doom in the teeth of the gale.

Half-mast hung the flag; and that other boat
Launched a small craft out on the waves afloat;
They watched the brave deed from the doomed ship there,
While over the sea rose a hope and a prayer, —

When, sudden as thought, the flag was gone !
Still the rescuers' boat toiled bravely on;
'T was madness to dare it, but hearts were brave,
With fellow-men prey to the merciless wave.

And so, through the fury that lashed the strand,
The little boat pressed with persistence grand ;
Ere the wreck went down they had saved the men,
And they questioned about the signal then.

" Why did you put your flag out of sight ? "
And the captain answered : " 'T was madness quite
For you to attempt a rescue here ;
We had no boats, and the end was near.

" We smothered our hopes; 't was a pity, we knew,
When we were drowning, to sacrifice you,
So we lowered our flag from its station high,
That you might be saved, though we must die."

———————

DIES IRÆ.

TRANSLATED BY THE REV. J. ANKETELL.

SEE, it dawns, that day of burning,
    Oft by king and prophet told ;
This fair earth to ashes turning,
    Flaming heavens together rolled,
        While the glittering
Banners of the Cross unfold !

Ah ! what terror is impending,
    When the Judge of man descends,
Strictly to our deeds attending,
    Every secret veil he rends,
        And the sinner
To His rod of justice bends.

Hark ! the trumpet's wondrous swelling
    Calls Death's captives from the ground,
Every dark sepulchral dwelling
    Echoes to its awful sound,
        And the legions
Of the dead, God's throne surround.

Death, amazed with sudden terror,
    Opens wide the mighty tomb :
Nature, owning human error,
    Hides her pallid face in gloom ;
        Man, the creature,
Rises to receive his doom.

Then a book of fiery pages
　Flashes on our startled eyes ;
All the sins of bygone ages
　Shall a guilty world surprise ;
　　While for refuge
All in vain the sinner cries.

When the Judge, from heaven descending,
　Mounts His crystal throne on high,
All His marshalled hosts attending,
　Flaming legions of the sky,
　　Nothing hidden
Shall escape His searching eye.

What shall I, frail man, be pleading?
　How from sin's sad doom be freed?
To what patron interceding,
　Begging him my cause to plead,
　　When the righteous
God's free grace for safety need?

King of majesty and glory,
　Who dost free salvation give,
Listen to Redemption's story,
　Bid Thy erring children live !
　　Fount of Pity,
Save me, and my sins forgive !

Holy Jesu, with compassion
　Think upon Thine earthly way,
How I caused Thy bitter Passion
　When in sin I went astray.
　　Blessed Saviour,
Leave me not in that dread day.

Weak and weary Thou hast sought me,
　Lost to God and dead to Thee :
With Thy Blood and Passion bought me,
　Hanging on th' accursed tree :
　　Let such labor
Not in vain be spent on me.

Righteous Judge of retribution,
  Who my guilt and woe didst bear,
Grant Thy gift of absolution
  To a trembling sinner's prayer;
    Lest I perish
In that hour of dark despair.

As a guilty culprit, groaning,
  Low I bend before Thy Throne,
Blushing, my transgressions owning —
  Sins for which Thou didst atone.
    Spare Thy suppliant;
Lord, I cling to Thee alone !

Thou, who Mary gav'st remission,
  When with tears she bathed Thy feet, —
Heard'st the dying thief's petition
  On the cross, Thy mercy-seat, —
    Hope hast given
That my pardon is complete.

Though my prayers are void of merit,
  Thy blest love can never tire ;
Let my soul in Thee inherit
  All Thy ransomed saints desire ;
    Save in mercy
From a doom of endless fire.

With Thy sheep a place provide me,
  Pastured in eternal light ;
From the guilty goats divide me,
  Banished from Thy blissful sight;
    On Thy right hand
Set me, clad in robes of white.

When with tears of bitter anguish
  To their doom the lost descend,
In eternal flames to languish,
  In a death that knows no end, —
    With the holy
Bid me to Thy joys ascend.

Low in prayer I bow before Thee,
  Prostrate in the very dust,
With a contrite heart implore Thee
  For a portion with the just ;
    In my death-pangs
  Let Thy mercy be my trust.

On that day of tears and terror
  Man, arising from his clay,
Stands accused of sin and error,
  Guilty, trembling with dismay.
    Holy Jesu
Save him in that awful day !

UNFINISHED.

By E. A. Clarke.

I WORKED at the task the Master
  Had set me at early morn,
When the earth lay fresh and glowing
  In the radiant light of dawn.

My hopes were fresh as the dewdrops,
  My heart as bright as the sun ;
I sang as I worked, and pictured
  The joy of a task well done.

But the day wore on, and the dewdrops
  Were kissed by the sun away ;
On my lips the song grew fainter
  I had chanted at break of day.

But the work was still the Master's,
  So I toiled with loving care
Though my hands grew weak and weary
  And my song became a prayer.

Then suddenly all around me
  A glad shout rings on high:
My comrade's task is completed!
  Can I join in the joyous cry?

I look at mine unfinished,
  I glance at the setting sun, —
Perhaps 't is an angel whispers,
  " 'T is the Master's work that is done."

So I blend my voice in the anthem
  Of praise for the work complete,
As 't is bought with reverent footsteps
  To lay at the Master's feet.

Then I turn alone in the shadows
  To work while the daylight last;
Did I fancy, or was it truly
  An angel that flitted past?

" Grieve not at thy work unfinished,"
  He whispered; " the Lord loves best,
The gift of a will submissive,
  And a heart in His love at rest."

VISIONS IN OAK HILL CEMETERY.

By F. Burge Griswold.

BROWN leaves upon the old oak trees,
  Melodious in the gentle breeze:

Snowdrops, with meek inclining heads
Beside the lowly, silent beds;

The yellow dandelion, king
Of all the early flowers of spring:

The crocus, with its petals bright,
Purple, and gold, and purest white ;

The shadow of a bird, that flies
Up toward the realms of Paradise ;

Bees, sipping from the blossoms spread
In sweet remembrance o'er the dead :

The marble monuments that keep
Their record while our dear ones sleep ;

The circling hills, the bending sky,
With benediction from on high, —

Such are the memories that embrace
That quiet, hallowed resting-place.

HEAVEN.

By the Rev. Cameron Mann.

" PRESS on to Heaven ! " — so goes the common
  speech —
" Cast loose from these foul noisy quays, and sail
For happy islands far beyond the reach
  Of this deceptive present, dark and stale."
Vain thoughts ! that eyes which see naught here shall hail
A joyous light on some untrodden beach ;
And what familiar voices could not teach
  In stately song of seraphs shall prevail.

The heavenly sunbeams on earth's highways fall,
  The blessed angels move through worldly din,
Not over seas but in the streets they call,
  At every step we meet celestial kin.
In sacramental parts is shown the All ;
  The gate to God stands open here, — press in !

RACINE REVISITED.

By the Rev. J. H. Knowles.

A H ! my dear DeKoven, slumber,
   Slumber 'neath thy granite cross;
Sleep in peace ! though we may never
   Cease to mourn thy bitter loss.

Sad it is to miss thy loved smile
   Welcoming our pilgrim feet,
Sad to know that we shall never
   Hear on earth thy accents sweet.

But the thought comes still to cheer us
   That thy work is being done,
That the spirit of the Master
   Rules from rise till set of sun.

In the silent grave thy body
   Lies beneath the carven stone,
But the sound of prayer and praises
   Echoes near with ceaseless tone.

In the place of the departed
   Rests in peace thy happy soul,
Waiting there, with prayerful spirit,
   For the Church's glorious goal.

Here on earth, before the altar
   Which thy saintly hands did rear.
In sweet union with thy soul's quest
   Rises still the voice of prayer.

Still at early hour that altar
   Is aglow with lights that shed
Beams of peace on those who offer
   Day by day the Mystic Bread.

Still the daily round of Matins
  Bright with all its surpliced throng,
Still the noonday Intercessions
  Lead us on to Evensong.

Still the sweet voice of the Warden
  Breathes o'er all the word of peace;
Ah! how good to know that God's work
  Never, never here shall cease.

Dear DeKoven, sweetly slumber,
  Slumber 'neath thy granite cross,
Sleep in peace! for time hath tempered
  Thy mysterious, long felt loss.

GORDON.

By R. H. G. O.

ENGLAND! thy days of glory are not o'er —
  For sure a nobler hero ne'er drew breath
Than dauntless Gordon, — in his life and death
Right worthy of the chivalry of yore.
No man he feared; but striding vanward, bore
God's banner on with an unflinching faith;
As though he heard with heaven-tunèd ear,
"Thus saith the Lord;" and hearing, cared for nothing
  more.

His memory is a trumpet, echoing down
Into the deepest caverns of the heart,
Where like a graven image Self is shrined;
Oh, weave for his dear head no funeral crown;
Drop but one tear, and turning to depart,
Seek thou to be like him in soul and mind.

"ST." AND "D. D."

BY THE AUTHOR OF "THE MOST NAMED CHURCH."

ONE Joseph Parker wrote a book,
  A famous book wrote he;
And on the titlepage he put
  That he was a " D. D."

Of great and worthy men he wrote —
  Of James and John and Paul,
But who they were, from any mark,
  You could not guess at all.

If James and John and Paul may not
  As " Saints " be known to fame,
Why does this Joseph Parker add
  " D. D." to his own name ?

MORNING.

BY THOMAS MAIR.

'TIS early morn! each trembling, dewy spray
  With radiant beauty glows within the light
That streams in splendor from the rising sun
  'Gainst the dark background of departing night.

O'er the broad bosom of the sparkling sea
  The foam-crowned billows haste to greet the shore,
With low-breathed murmurs of the lapping tide,
  That speak of peace and joy forevermore.

Thro' the dark wood and o'er the sunlit plain,
  The feathered songsters pour their hymn of praise;
While gentle breezes, wandering thro' the grove,
  Join the sweet anthem that their voices raise.

Earth in her beauty draws so near to heaven,
　We seem to dwell within its blessed peace;
When in our hearts all pain and grief depart,
　And God has bid the mourner's tear to cease.

Will such a morning break upon my soul,
　When God shall call my spirit from earth's night,
To dwell forever in a deeper gloom
　Or wake to endless glory in His sight?

His will be done! But when life's path grows dark,
　When doubt and trial rest upon my way,
E'en in the gloom I hear my Saviour's voice
　And know His hand will guide me when I stray.

So in His love I wait, with trusting heart,
　To see the shadows break and flee away,
When in the sunshine of His gracious smile
　My night shall vanish in eternal day.

EVENING.

By Thomas Mair.

HOW calm the wooded hills repose
　Beneath the softened light,
Reflected from the glowing clouds
　That mark Aurora's flight.

The radiant masses, piled on high,
　With wondrous beauty gleam,
As if already on their brows
　Heaven's opening glories beam.

No sound the holy stillness breaks,
　Save when the murmuring pine
Utters its anthem in the breeze,
　To nature's Lord divine.

In such an hour my spirit turns
From all its worldly care,
And feels within its longing soul
God's holy presence there.

My listening ears can almost catch
The hymn of Heaven's bright choir;
My eyes, that pierce the radiant blue,
Reflect my heart's desire.

When will the cords that bind to earth
Break, and my spirit free!
O Lord, 't is weary waiting here,
I long for Heaven and Thee.

GOLDEN-ROD.

By the Rev. Hobart B. Whitney.

ON the river bank reclining,
Where no noisy footsteps trod,
Thoughts and cares of life resigning,
There we gathered golden-rod.

There no sounds of toil were straying,
There no laborers strive and plod;
But of merry children playing,
Where we gathered golden-rod.

Woodland scents were soft distilling,
Breathing from the fragrant sod:
Woodland sounds the air were filling,
Where we gathered golden-rod.

In the zephyrs — going — coming —
There the wood-weeds sway and nod;
Drowsy bees were softly humming,
Where we gathered golden-rod.

And the autumn seeds were scattering,
   Showering from the bursting pod ;
And the trembling leaves were chattering
   Where we gathered golden-rod.

Through the trees the sun-rays sifting
   Danced like fairies golden-shod ;
Golden clouds above were drifting,
   Where we gathered golden-rod.

And the river, calmly flowing,
   Seemed the benison of God ;
Gate of Heaven, — the sunset glowing,
   Where we gathered golden-rod !

THE MESSAGE OF LOVE.

By H. P. Huse.

I HAD a message sent to me once
   From a country over the sea,
So sweet, so strange, that I could not guess
   Who sent that message to me.
They said that it came from Christ the Lord
   Who lived in Galilee ;
And all that He said was, " Love," still love ;
   And so was His message to me.

" Love ye one another," — thus it came
   From that Holy Land over the sea, —
" So men shall know that ye are mine,
   For loving them ye love me."
And " Even as I love you, love them,"
   Was the message to you and to me ;
Do you think we try to *live* these words
   That were spoken in Galilee ?

THE SONG OF SPRING.

By J. W. P.

COME with garlands fresh and fair,
  To wreathe the gladsome year:
To sound a watchword through the
    land:
  " Brothers, be of good cheer ! "

I come to chase the gloom away
  Of sterile winter's hand;
To scatter brightness as the day
  O'er every vernal land.

I come to visit earth again,
  With sunshine and with shower;
Imparting to the faithful soil
  The secret of my power.

I come to play a wizard's part
  With birds and beasts and flowers,
To thrill dead nature into life,
  And wake her dormant powers.

I come to pour my odors forth
  Upon the zephyr wind:
And paint my colors, rich and rare,
  On every flower I find.

I come to fill the woods and groves
  With music ever true,
And teach the great cathedral choir
  Their anthems to renew.

I come to move the finny tribe
  To sportive gambols free,
Making the bright and sparkling brook
  To dance with ecstasy.

I come to lighten human woe,
  The sufferer to ease,
To kiss the cheek and make it glow
  With health and joy and peace.

I come that charter to renew,
  Of ages long ago, —
" Seed time and harvest, cold and heat,
  No more shall earth forego."

I come to cheer the fainting soul,
  By my perennial youth,
With visions of a spring to come —
  A resurrection truth.

I come to teach the sons of men
  A faithful Father's love,
And lead them in true thankfulness
  To raise their hearts above.

———————

A NOBLE RIDE.

By L.

A DOWN the hill he rode :
  Not for his noble blood
  Shall he be known ;
Not for an ancient name,
Shall his undying fame
  Be proudly sung.

Into the town he rode :
On came the mighty flood,
  As he rode on.
" Run to the hills ! " he cried :
" Turn to the mountain side !
  My brothers, run ! "

17

Through street and lane with speed,
He dashed his frantic steed:
    His cry rang out:
" Run to the hills!" They turned
To see if he were mad, then learned
    The meaning of that shout.

The mighty flood came on!
Rider and horse went down,
    Their work at end.
The flood swept cruelly by,
A bitter, wailing cry
    The people send.

Too late they understand
The rider's brief command:
    " Run to the hills!"
But he had done his best.
God grant him peace and rest,
    Beyond all ills.

"VAIN IS THE HELP OF MAN."

BY RICA H. FINLAY.

OTHER friends may come and go;
    Thou shalt fail me never;
On Thy faithful, tender love,
    May I lean forever.

Never shall I ask in vain;
    Thou art ever willing
To fulfil my soul's request,
    All its trouble stilling.

Earthly friend can never meet
  All my heart's deep yearning;
To a Love omnipotent
  It is ever turning.

As the flower turns to the sun,
  Source of all its beauty;
So my spirit ever yields
  To the Lord her duty.

Mortal cannot live without
  Homage to his Maker, —
Of all joys and hopes of men
  Giver and Partaker.

Vain it is to seek on earth
  Lasting peace or gladness :
All its joys, and all its hopes
  Only end in sadness.

Let our aching, yearning hearts
  Raise their longing higher,
And to purer, better joys
  Let our souls aspire, —

Seek to live at peace with God,
  Seek to lay up treasure
Where our souls at last shall find
  Joy that hath no measure.

THE UNREAL AND THE REAL.

BY THE REV. GEO. M. EVERHART, D. D.

IN the hills from my window fair Pisgah is seen,
  The Queen of the mountains, in beauty and sheen ;
'T is said she is robed by Distance, her maid,
In vesture of blue 'neath the light and the shade.

Enchanting, the mountains are ever the same,
With Distance to robe them, with fancy aflame ;
But disrobe them of azure, come near to their breast,
And alas ! riven rocks, torn limbs, from their crest,
Ravines in their sides and dead wood from their trees,
And wild brush, and rents, and all else you may please,
Disclose the old mountain to be but a fraud —
A monster at home, an angel abroad.

The beauty of form and the colors of light
That symbolize life in its sensuous delight,
Are parts of the world — the butterfly glow —
They enchain us awhile till we grasp them and know
That skeleton forms of sorrows within,
And all the array of earth's troubles and sin
Make life as it is — make life in the real,
Unmasking the false, the true to reveal.

But there are mountains beyond, green hills far away,
Where the vesture is golden or azure by day,
The shadows of twilight but soften the scene,
The clouds never burst, yet the hillsides are green.
Adown over sands as white as the snow,
Leaps onward the fountain with rhythmical flow ;
The velvet-like grass and the beautiful flower
Make the near and the far of magnetical power.

And is it not true that in life may be found
The noble and good in whom truth may abound ?
That the glitter of fraud does in no way prevail
To blind them with folly, their spirits assail,
But that near to such souls are the virtues of heaven,
And to God, as their All, their whole life has been given ?

A HYMN.

By Mary C. Preston.

HOW long, O Lord, how long?
The glory and the song
That shone and sounded at Thy birth
Grow dim and faint throughout the fainting earth :
And heavily falls the doom of death,
And all our hope still tarrieth.

How long, O Lord, how long?
The weary ages throng
With wail of birth and wail of dying;
The prayers of ages wait replying:
Time holds his throne, the graves still keep
Their dead, and still the living weep.

How long, O Lord, how long?
Arise, O Great and Strong,
And quit at last the heavenly places.
Begirt with glory-clouds and angel faces,
Break through the spaces of the golden stars,
And loose eternally our prison bars !

LINES TO A CHALICE TWICE RESCUED FROM THE FLAMES.

By the Rev. F. W. Taylor, S. T. D.

BLEST token of the dying love of Christ !
Dear symbol of His awful sacrifice !
Pledge of His conflict in Gethesemane !
Chalice of blessing, filled from Jesu's side !
Thy charmed existence tells the faithful tale,
That he who searcheth for the Holy Grail,

And marks his pathway by the mystic light
That gently falls upon his anxious sight,
Must tread 'mid flames consuming, fierce, and wild,
As pure and single-hearted as a child ;
Must haste to midnight risk, when praise has ceased,
As watchful as the consecrated priest.
    They bear to fainting men
    The Cup of Life again,
    When fiery wrath and death
    Encompass all beneath, —
They, most like children, most like priests of God,
Who scathless 'midst the world's dread fires have trod.

IMPRISONED.

By L. L. ROBINSON.

SHUT in ?   Ah, no ! we call not them shut in
   Whose busy hearts with folded hands must lie,
Hearing afar the world's low, muffled din,
   Or hushed at night on tip-toe passing by ;
Ah, no ! such souls are free to soar afar,
While they who near them watch oft prisoned are.

Shut in ?   Ah, no ! not they whose yearning gaze
   Meets only mighty hills on every side,
That softly veil within their silvery haze
   The world, whose visage sad 't were well to hide :
Ah, no ! souls thus shut in scale heights unknown
To many a crown upon an earthly throne.

Then who are they whom we should call shut in ?
   They only who within the hardened shell
Of *self* fast prisoned are ; who, looking in,
   Or out, or up, see naught but their own cell :
Whose highest aim self's highest greed to win, —
These are the souls whom we should call *shut in.*

FAITH AND WORKS.

BY BROOKS O. BAKER.

TWO persons met each Sunday morn
    To cross the river Tay,
Where each his own opinion taught
    In a dogmatic way.
The ferryman, a knowing Scot,
    Each Sunday heard them say
No mortal man could e'er be saved,
    Outside a certain way.
One said 't was faith, and faith alone,
    Could ever save a man,
And every one will be condemned
    Who tries another plan.
The other held it was by works,
    That faith alone was dead,
That works would save the righteous man, —
    " Good works will save," he said.
On Sunday morn, when half way o'er,
    The ferry-boat went round,
And though it went quite rapidly,
    It got no nearer ground.
" Put out the other oar," one said :
    The boatman did obey,
But still no progress did they make —
    They went the other way.
Then the divines were sore annoyed
    To see the trick he played :
" Work both together," they command ;
    The boatman then obeyed.
On went the boat, and quickly too,
    As if 't were in a race,
And safely brought the worthy crew
    Unto their landing-place.
" Well, gentlemen," the boatman said,
    " What have I done this morn ? "

" You 've wasted time in turning round ! "
  They answered him with scorn.
" Just look ! " the wily Scotchman said,
  " The name 's upon each oar.
Whene'er I pulled with Faith or Works,
  We got no nearer shore ;
'T was only when I worked the two
  The boat had any go ;
And you will find that Faith and Works
  Must pull together so."

THE SISTER.

BY THE REV. F. W. TAYLOR, S. T. D.

A LIFE of peace, all calm within ; without,
  All active duty ; love's pure service given ;
A faith so warm no chilling winds of doubt
  Can bar with clouds her intercourse with Heaven.

A life of prayer, thus love breathes forth, to Love
  Divine and boundless, every deep desire ;
And each rapt soul, enkindled from above,
  Mingles her incense with Heaven's altar fire.

And still more precious fruit of Cavalry's Tree
  Is garnered in Heaven's storehouse by her King ;
Better than costliest sacrifice, the free
  Obedience Christ's hallowed Bride doth bring.

O Blessed Jesu ! teach Thy doubting Church
  How rich the grace Thou hast on her bestowed.
Bid her faint heart take courage, and the torch
  Of Love re-lit to clasp, and praise her God.

THE TOKEN.

BY THE REV. WILLIAM FRANCIS DICKENSON, M. D.

[At the Consecration of Bishop Potter in Grace Church, New York, just after the laying on of hands, a ray of sunlight shone through the storm then prevailing.]

THE services began in tempest loud,
    And deluges of rain which swept the streets;
The heavens were wrapped in sombre-mantled cloud.
    Against the windows dashed the bleak stormbeats.

The organ prelude rolled its thunders sweet
    While robed processions moved along the aisle, —
Elders, Apostles, who with peace-shod feet
    Had gathered here in greeting for awhile

Of him, elect Apostle, now so soon
    To stand with Christ's commission given,
In all the fulness of his life's rich noon,
    "A legate of the skies " — an officer of Heaven.

There were Christ's ministers from far and wide:
    Among the wisest, noblest, and the best,
From the far East, from Rocky Mountains' side —
    The fair Southland, the prairies of the West.

The solemn services were finished now,
    Which led up to the final, crowning act —
" The laying on of hands."   Then came the vow :
    " A shepherd of the flock, the faith intact,

" I promise faithfully to be — to keep;
    In tenderness and love to wield the rod,
Remembering all Christ's poor, weak, straying sheep ;
    Not done alone, but with the help of God."

The mitred leaders, as the questions ceased,
  In solemn readiness there waiting stood,
And spake the words by which the kneeling priest
  Should rise a bishop in the Church of God.

" We lay our hands in delegated power
  Upon thy head.   Now in the saintly line
Henceforth and ever from this solemn hour,
  A bishop's oversight and work are thine.

" Nor let this sacred charge from thee depart;
  O Watchman. Leader, faithful at thy post!
Ever God's gift keep glowing in thy heart,
  And for this work, ' Receive the Holy Ghost.' "

The words were ended, when, behold, a wave
  Of sunlight 'mid the storm came floating down
Through the rich panes, and lit the hallowed nave,
  As if in storm and shine were mingled cross and crown.

Mark this glad token, herald of the cross!
  Shine forth in splendor through life's gloom and sin!
Amid its cloud and storm, its pain and loss,
  Thou mitred Leader, stand, in heaven's own sheen!

THE SISTER'S VOW.

LINES ADDRESSED TO A MOTHER SUPERIOR.

By A.

DEAR, gentle eyes in which I see
    A reflex of the Love divine!
Dear, steadfast hand that holdest me!
And dear, calm heart that strengthenest mine!

O Mother! 't is an easy task
To thee my threefold vow to make;
Here let me kneel, and, fervent, ask
To keep it for a Dearer's sake.

Weary at last of wandering,
Now will I rest, and count it sweet
My hands, and head, and heart to bring,
And lay them at the Master's Feet.

O Mother! take forevermore
This wayward will that would not break,
This passionate love that would not soar,
And guide, and raise, for Jesu's sake!

STILL RING THE BELLS.

By H. C. McKeever.

IN pride of human reason,
    Men scale the lofty sky,
And with a sacrilegious hand
    The God of heaven defy;
Would dig, and analyze, and sift
    Each little grain of dust,
Till baffled, 'gainst an iron wall
    Of darkness, bow they must.
And *yet* the spires point up to heaven,
And still the bells ring grandly on.

Out of the caverns cold and drear
    Crowds of dark spirits creep,
Quenching the star of Christian hope
    In death's eternal sleep,

Casting a pall of darkest gloom
  O'er man's mysterious fate,
Beating against the iron bars
  With frantic blows of hate.
And *yet* the spires point up to heaven.
And still the bells ring grandly on.

Spreading the fogs of unbelief
  O'er weak and trembling hearts,
Dimming the starry light of truth,
  Piercing with cruel darts
The humble souls that look to heaven
  For light, and joy, and peace,
Tearing away the feeble hope
  That longs for sweet release.
And *yet* the spires point up to heaven,
And still the bells ring grandly on.

What will they do with Jesus Christ,
  Who with majestic tread
Is walking through the centuries,
  Heaven shining overhead?
" Lo! I am with you to the end,"
  Has every cavil still'd. —
The power of every precious word
  Still day by day fulfill'd.
And *yet* the spires point up to heaven,
And still the bells ring grandly on.

For eighteen hundred rolling years,
  Through seas of blood and strife,
While earthly kingdoms wax and wane,
  The Lord of endless life
Is marching on to take His throne,
  To conquer all his foes:
To crown his saints with victory,
  To heal His people's woes.
And *yet* the spires point up to heaven,
And still the bells ring grandly on.

Up from the depth of Christian hearts
   There comes the voice of faith :
Heaven-sent, heaven-kept, it answers back,
   For "thus my Master saith."
Doubters may fling their scornful sneers,
   We *feel* that Christ is near ;
Down in the castle of the heart,
   We *know* that He is here.
And *yet* the spires point up to heaven,
And still the bells ring grandly on.

Here, in the grand cathedral choir,
   Here, in the lowly fane,
Where God's dear children worship Him
   In love's most raptured strain :
Here, in the countless homes of rest,
   For weary ones of earth, —
For all the sheltering arms of love
   From Him must date their birth.
And *yet* the spires point up to heaven,
And still the bells ring grandly on.

Here, in the witnesses for Him, —
   The homes for lame and blind,
The orphan and the Magdalen,
   All sorts of humankind ;
In feeble copies of our Lord,
   In voices sweet and clear,
His people witness to the truth
   That Jesus Christ is *here.*
And *yet* the spires point up to heaven,
And still the bells ring grandly on.

No wonder that the hosts of hell
   Are rallying to the fight ;
When through the twilight of the past,
   Beyond the dreary night,
We see the rosy dawn of day
   Above the eastern seas, —

Light from the Orient !   Life from death !
    Come wafted on the breeze.
And *yet* the spires point up to heaven,
And still the bells ring grandly on.

    You cannot still these Gospel bells,
        Nor tear the temple down ;
    You cannot crush these lofty spires,
        Nor trample Jesus' crown.
    For on, and on, the bells will ring,
        Till nations from afar
    Shall echo back the blessed chimes
        That hail the " Morning Star."
And *yet* the spires point up to heaven,
And still the bells ring grandly on.

    The bells of the Nativity
        Proclaim that He is here :
    The tables spread with Jesus' love
        Our waiting spirits cheer, —
    Waiting throughout the centuries
        For Christ to claim His own,
    When in His glorious majesty,
        He takes His righteous throne.
And *yet* the spires point up to heaven,
And still the bells ring grandly on.

MY CABIN.

By Elsie White Gaynor.

THE winter's wind is blowing chill,
    It seeks an entrance at door and sill,
But my well-built cabin
And hearth aglow
Are sure defence from any foe.

The world, they say, is full of strife.
Yet mine is a quiet and peaceful life,
For my well-built cabin
And hearth aglow
Are faithfullest of friends, I trow.

The world is full of anxious care
For goods and gold I do not share,
For my well-built cabin
And hearth aglow
Are all I need and all I know.

And the world is full of bitter loss,
Where men count store their worthless dross,
But my well-built cabin
And hearth aglow
A portion are that brings no woe.

Could the world but taste of a humbler life,
Forget its pomp and ambitious strife,
My well-built cabin
And hearth aglow
And their quiet, peace, and comfort know!

But the world will scoff at my simple pride,
My humbler pleasures it will deride ;
And my well-built cabin
And hearth aglow
And the joys they bring it will never know.

SUNSET THOUGHTS.

BY JOSEPHINE SMITH WOOD.

THE western glow of amber bright,
    Floods all the land with golden light:
A fleecy cloud, just tinged with red,
Like burnished fret-work hangs o'erhead.

The gorgeous sky in sunset drest
Is mirrored on the calm sea's breast:
A far-off gleaming sail doth lend
Its beauty to the day's sweet end.

Naught now is heard save muffled roar
Of restless wave-beat on the shore ;
And musing thoughts within me rise,
That fill with tears my grateful eyes.

The heavenly country seems to me
To lie beyond that sunlit sea ;
These waters, stilled at His command,
Are " in the hollow of His hand."

Thy way, O Lord, permits no flaw,
The best *comes last* — such is Thy law.
The fairest sky lies in the west ;
'T is at the close of day we rest.

The dying year doth earth enfold,
With scarlet robe and cloth of gold ;
And lengthened shadows softest seem,
When twilight silvers all the stream.

So time the sharp edge roundeth o'er,
Which hurt us once and wounded sore ;
Its mellow light doth faults obscure —
Were it not so, who could endure !

Like this fair day I find complete,
I know life's close shall be as sweet ;
For light will be its eventide,
With heavenly portals opening wide.

And when for me life's day is past,
May my expectant soul, at last,
Bathe in the golden light, outpoured
From that fair city of our Lord.

The sunset fades, but morn comes fair ;
The dead year doth a Spring prepare ;
And so my soul, from its dead clay,
Shall waken, satisfied, some day.

PSALM XXIII.

By the Rev. John Milton Peck.

THE Lord, my God, in pastures green,
　In fertile fields He placeth me;
My Shepherd King, by brooklet sheen,
　Without a lack, He feedeth me.

And when my soul hath gone astray,
　Then to the right He turneth me;
And ever in the righteous way,
　Oh, bless His Name! He leadeth me.

Yea, e'en when death's dark shadows come,
　I'll know no fear — He holdeth me;
His presence then shall bear me home,
　His rod and staff shall comfort me.

And with a ready table spread,
　Against my foes He shieldeth me;
With holy oil upon my head,
　And cup of joy, He filleth me.

Goodness and mercy all my days,
  From my dear Lord, shall follow me ;
And in His house, with ceaseless praise,
  I 'll dwell, — my God, He knoweth me.

LITTLE MARJORIE'S LOVE STORY.

By MARGUERITE BOUVET, Author of "Sweet William." Fully illustrated by Helen Maitland Armstrong. Small 4to, $1.25.

MISS BOUVET'S popularity as a writer for the young was at once established on the publication of her first and very successful book, "Sweet William." Her new book, "Little Marjorie's Love Story," cannot fail to be equally popular. The unselfish love of plain, timid Little Marjorie for her beautiful, gifted, imperious brother, and his denial of her when at the zenith of his career, at a time when he was carrying peace and comfort to the souls of hundreds by the angel-like sweetness of his voice, is told with that charm which Miss Bouvet possesses in such a singular degree. The beauty and pathos of the story are touching, and the delicate way in which the characteristics of the one child are contrasted with those of the other is as effective as the lights and shadows of a picture. Pride and selfishness never seemed more contemptible than in the person of the handsome Gerald, nor unselfish love and self-sacrificing sisterly devotion more beautiful than in that of sweet little Marjorie. The illustrator, Miss Armstrong, has told the story in picture as effectively as the author has in words.

Sold by all booksellers, or mailed, on receipt of price, by

A. C. McCLURG AND CO., Publishers,

Cor. Wabash Ave. and Madison St., Chicago.

Sweet William.

By Marguerite Bouvet. With Illustrations by Helen and Margaret Armstrong. Small quarto, 209 pages, $1.50.

This very attractive little volume is unlike any other book we can think of. It takes us back to mediæval times, and introduces us to the lords and ladies who then inhabited the splendid castle that still looks down from the heights of Mount St. Michael, on the coast of Normandy. It tells the pathetic story (with a happy ending) of a little boy, who had he lived to-day would have been a genuine Little Lord Fauntleroy, and introduces us also to a Little Lady Fauntleroy, with whom we cannot help falling in love. The illustrations are singularly beautiful and appropriate, and make it altogether one of the most attractive juvenile books of recent years.

———◆———

For sale by booksellers generally, or will be sent, post-paid, on receipt of the price, by

A. C. McCLURG AND CO., Publishers,
CHICAGO.

A Song of Life.

By MARGARET WARNER MORLEY. With profuse Illustrations by the Author and by Robert Forsyth. Price, $1.25.

THE plan and purpose of this work are at once very unusual and admirable. A special student of biology and embryology and a charming writer, the author also possesses the rare combination of scientific, literary, and artistic attainments which render such a work posssible.

It unfolds the mystery of plant and animal existence with a charm of manner and delicacy of treatment that delight while they instruct. Mothers who read it will quickly see its value and will gladly put it into the hands of their sons and daughters, to whom its beautiful and significant "Song of Life" will hardly be sung in vain.

———◆———

For sale by booksellers generally, or will be sent, post-paid, on receipt of the price, by

A. C. McCLURG AND CO., Publishers,
CHICAGO.

THE STORY OF TONTY.

An Historical Romance. By MARY HARTWELL
CATHERWOOD, author of "The Romance of
Dollard," "The Lady of Fort St. John," etc.
Profusely Illustrated from original drawings by
Mr. Enoch Ward. 12mo, 224 pages, $1.25.

"THE Story of Tonty," in which Mrs. Catherwood's genius
for historical romance reaches perhaps its highest manifestation,
is a Western story, beginning at Montreal, tarrying at Fort
Frontenac, and ending at the old fort at Starved Rock, on the
Illinois river. It weaves the adventures of the two great ex-
plorers, the intrepid La Salle and his faithful lieutenant, Tonty,
into a tale as thrilling and romantic as the descriptive portions
are brilliant and vivid. It is superbly illustrated with twenty-
three masterly drawings by Mr. Enoch Ward.

———•———

*For sale by booksellers generally, or will be sent, post-paid, on
receipt of the price, by*

A. C. McCLURG AND CO., Publishers,
CHICAGO.